I0123437

SERIAL GOOD SAMARITAN

By

Jeanne "Bean" Murdock

Copyright © Jeanne "Bean" Murdock 2021
BEANFIT Publishing
Paso Robles, CA
USA

Copyright © Jeanne "Bean" Murdock 2021
All rights reserved.
This book may not be reproduced, in whole or in part, including
illustrations, in any form (beyond that copying permitted by
Sections 107 and 108 of the US Copyright Law and except by
reviewers for the public press), without written permission from
the author.

Library of Congress Control Number: 2021907009
ISBN: 978-0977067862

Some of the names in this book have been changed for privacy.
There is an asterisk (*) after one's pseudonym the first time the
name is mentioned.

Cover image by Jeanne Murdock.
Vietnam Women's Memorial, Washington, DC.
Sculptor: Glenna Goodacre.

Back cover image by Jim Tyler.

All interior images are by Jeanne Murdock unless otherwise
stated.
Each image complements the story that follows it.

I dedicate this book to everyone who breaks their schedule to stop and help someone or an animal.

TABLE OF CONTENTS

INTRODUCTION

I was in Girl Scouts from Kindergarten through 5th grades. From the beginning, one of the good deeds we were taught was to help senior citizens cross the street. I was immediately hooked on that idea. I loved seniors and sought old people to help across the street. Can you imagine a 5-year-old child asking a senior if he needs help across the street?! That was me. And senior could mean only 65 years old!

As a child I also enjoyed helping my friends. I quickly learned two important qualities, particularly when their need was emotional support: listening and making people laugh. I remember when Gary* told me that his dog was hit and killed by a car, when Melanie* told me that her mom drank too much alcohol, when Lila* told me that her parents were getting divorced, and when Maya* told me her parents died. I felt like my elementary school's confidant.

I started teaching swimming lessons (for pay) when I was 17 years old. One way that I was a serial Good Samaritan was by saving *many* children from drowning. Rescues go along with being a swimming instructor. There's no Purple Heart award, no Medal of Freedom, and no Key to the City for these acts; it's just part of the job. You see, I normally had a class of six students at a time. I would make them hold onto the wall in deep (for them) water, so that their arms would get stronger. I would take one child at a time away from the wall to practice a skill. The impatient, fearless children would let go of the wall and try unsuccessfully to swim. I'd have to rush back to the wall, a child in tow, and pull the other child up from underwater and re-attach him to the wall.

1

A requirement for teaching swimming lessons is CPR. During a CPR class, I was given a one-inch-by-one-inch hard plastic container with a CPR mask (a thin, plastic film). I still have it; I've kept it in my purse for decades. You can infer that I've never used it; in other words, I wouldn't re-use it and, believe it or not, this serial Good Samaritan has not administered CPR in a real-life situation, yet.

In college I was normally the designated driver on a night out with friends, because *someone* had to protect them during inebriation. We couldn't all be drunk. Someone had to be the protector. So, did I hold my girlfriends' hair at the end of the night when they puked in the toilet? Hell no! I'm no Florence Nightingale. Besides, I have no sympathy for how people feel after they drink alcohol.

Since Kindergarten I have made it my mission not only to help seniors cross the street but also to help seniors in any way I can. I went on to make a career of working with seniors, my favorite demographic. Furthermore, the Girl Scouts lesson was more than just helping seniors cross the street. I knew that being a good person meant helping anyone anytime. Now in my 50s, I know that we are on Earth to learn while helping others during their spiritual journeys.

Enjoy this book. If a story doesn't fit your definition of Good Samaritan, then that's OK. Enjoy the story, anyway.

I hope you're left inspired to help others, to help strangers, to look for people and animals to help—daily— and to leave people with a tool to help themselves in the future. Lead with love, compassion, and grace.

My Wishes for the children of the World

My Wishes for the Children that are crippled are that people could make medicine to cure their disease. If there was a cure for diseases crippled people could have an operation. If someone was deaf or blind they should all have someone to help them get around.

I think that if we have a sister or a brother we should love them, and that we who have brothers and sisters should be grateful we do.

If someone fell down we should help them up and be a friend.

I think that nobody should pollute or make the air black. We should keep the air clean for not only the children in the world but for everybody that is living right now! Or we love we have to care for someone, to help them in any way we can.

On the previous page is a paper I wrote January 25, 1979, while in fifth grade.

My Wishes for Children of the World
[unedited]

My wishes for the children that are crippled, are that people could make medicine to cure their disease. If there was a cure for diseases crippled people could have an operation. If someone was deaf or blind they should all have someone help them get around.

I think that if we have a sister or a brother we should love them and that we who have brothers or/and sisters should be grateful we do.

If someone fell down we should help them up and be a friend.

I think that nobody should pollute or make the air black. We should keep the air clean for not only the children in the world but for everybody that is living right now!

To me Love means to care for someone, to help them in any way we can.

CHAPTER 1

ANIMALS

I'm not going to lie. I don't love all animals. I can't stand cats. What don't I like about cats? It's easier to tell you what I like about them: . . . .
A mourning dove's coo drives me cuckoo, especially if it's keeping me awake.

My favorite animal is the blue whale, and I LOVE dogs. I have reunited *many* lost dogs with their owners; not all of the dogs were happily reconnected. There's always a logical reason why dogs run away from home. "But dogs are loyal!" you cry. I used to think that until I was taught the reality: Dogs want food and shelter (emotional and physical). If you can't provide both, then they will take off when given the opportunity, no matter how much you "love" them.

I consider myself a dog whisperer. Through touch, mainly, I sense what the dog is experiencing emotionally and physically. Yes, animals have emotions. I have provided physical and psychological comfort to dogs and have healed them physically. I don't label myself as a medical intuitive or healer, because there is too much risk and potentially false hope in those claims. All I can guarantee is that I provide THE BEST dog massages and that the dog *always* gives me information.

One down one to go

   I was at an art gallery where the manager, Sally*, brought her two Boston terriers to hang out. She kept them tied to a railing just inside the front door. I was there helping an artist client of mine. At the end of the evening, Sally noticed that someone came in and stole the petty cash. Sally called the police and during the commotion one of the dogs wriggled loose of its collar and ran off. Since Sally was distracted by the theft, it took her a while to notice that the dog was missing. When she realized only one dog was by the front door, she became hysterical. I looked around the gallery and outside, called the dog, but I didn't see it. I told myself: Stop. Think like a dog. What does a dog want? What motivates a dog to obey? So, I untied the dog still at the front door, told someone to tell Sally that I took the dog, and walked through the gallery saying, "Alright. We're going for a walk. We'll see you later." Immediately, the lost dog sprinted out of one of the nooks. He was clearly thinking: *Walk? Walk! Don't go without me. Take me, too!*

Jump!

I was on a walk and saw a baby bird on the side of the road by itself. It was pacing in the street alongside the curb. Its demise was surely near, whether by car or predator.

I am a little skittish about touching animals, partly a tactile issue and partly I don't want them to give me a disease. I put my feet behind the chick; my heels were touching each other with my feet forming a 90-degree angle facing the curb. I cornered the chick so that the only direction it could go was up. I wasn't sure if it didn't know which direction to go or if it didn't have the strength to jump onto the curb. I sided with nature and scared the chick just enough for instinct and reflex to kick in. It jumped onto the curb and ran off into a bush. Success!

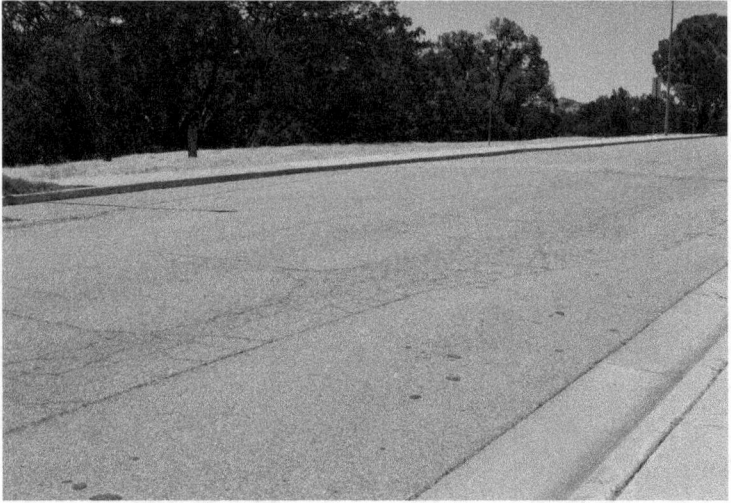

Fawn-dly, Jeanne

I was driving in a neighborhood and saw a fawn lying in the middle of the road. I could see that it was alive, but I didn't know if it were injured or resting from learning how to walk.

I pulled over and walked up to it. "Are you OK?" It stood up. "Are you hurt? You need to get out of the road." It quickly walked across the street and lay down in weeds, camouflaged. "Where's Mama?" I looked around and didn't see any other deer. I decided optimistically that the fawn would be reunited with the rest of the family and I turned to go back to my car.

Half-way across the street, I was met by a huge doe. We met eyes. I could hear it asking, "Where's my baby? Did you hurt my baby?" I said, "I come in peace. I'm one with nature. She's in the weeds." I left.

I keep in my head the line from Chiffon Margarine commercial: "It's not nice to fool Mother Nature." My version: "It's not nice to fool with Mother Nature."

Me with Shade
Photo courtesy of Shade's owner

Dogs grieve, too

I went to a hospital late one evening to visit a client. Afterward when I was back in the lobby, I felt like I needed comfort. It was almost time for bed, but I needed a release, someone to talk to so that I could let go of my client's emotion that I took on.

There were two people with a dog in the lobby. A dog! Just what I needed. I walked over and said hello. It turned out that the man owned the dog and he was with his elderly mother waiting for her husband to die. So sad. I asked if I could sit with them. They graciously said yes, and we had a nice chat.

I noticed that the dog, Shade, a black lab/pit bull mix was on a seat, restless and trying to sleep. I asked if I could pet the dog. The owner said absolutely, and I went to work. Shade told me that he was exhausted and sad; I told his owner. You know how sometimes you're so exhausted that you can't sleep? That's how the dog was. Through thought I told Shade that it was OK for him to let go of worry for his family. Meanwhile, I worked my magic massaging him and helping him to sleep. Within two minutes Shade was out cold and stayed asleep after I spent five minutes working on him.

So, did I get *my* release? No one worked on me physically or emotionally, directly. I certainly didn't pass on my pain to the dog as therapy dogs are accustomed to receiving. But as I illustrate in this book, helping others is incredibly cathartic.

Most people shouldn't own a dog

I was driving one evening on a quiet 4-lane road by a shopping center when I saw a young man dragging a pit bull out of the middle of the street and onto the sidewalk. After I drove by, I made a U-turn and parked along the street. It turned out that the dog had just been hit by a car and the man saw it happen while he was walking. The man didn't want the dog to be hit again.

Two other cars pulled over—two women—and we had a total of four of us humans and one dog. One woman hit the dog and the other had seen that dog and another running all over playing. The second woman was trying to corral the dogs when she saw the first lady hit one of the dogs.

I comforted and counseled everyone, each stressed for a different reason. I also treated the man, because he was badly bitten on the hand by the frightened dog. I made the dog lie down and tried to keep it still. It wanted to run off, but couldn't really. Its head was bloody and its back legs were in bad shape. The dog was so terrified that I wasn't able to keep it calm.

A policeman showed up and then animal control. The animal control officer plopped the dog on a stretcher and then put it in her truck. Yes, I said plopped. I wasn't impressed with her lack of gentleness. The dog was taken to the animal hospital.

One by one, I made sure everyone was "OK to leave." I said bye to the woman who hit the dog. I said bye to the woman who tried to corral the dogs. I said bye to the man and told him to go to the ER. He needed to know if he were at risk for rabies and if one of his fingers were broken.

The next day I called the animal hospital to ask about the dog, even though I knew the worker couldn't give out confidential information. She said that the dog was chipped and the owner was located. The worker wouldn't tell me if the dog survived, but I felt sure it didn't. I assumed the other dog made it home safely that night.

There are dog owners who open the front door of their homes to let dogs out for exercise. The owners are too lazy to take the dogs for a walk. "The dogs will come back when they're hungry or tired." Or, the dogs will return in a body bag. I hope that the dog owner in this story was placed in the middle of a street in front of a moving vehicle.

Choke, Mommy

A friend gave me a few gifts to give to my dogs. One gift was a bag of pig ears. Gross. Since my dogs, chocolate lab/Australian shepherd mixes, ate anything and everything, I figured that they would enjoy the treats.

I gave one to Tommy and one to Cammy. I put Tommy outside, since he normally ate his treats fast and then would steal Cammy's. Cammy was in the dining room eating, and I was in my office. Moms, you know how you always know what your kids are doing, especially when they are hurt? I had one of those moments.

I stopped hearing Cammy SLOP SLOP SLOP. I went to check on him and he was not breathing. He was choking on the ear! Cammy was still conscious, still standing, and exhibiting the gag reflex. I straddled his body, felt for the base of his rib cage, and performed the Heimlich maneuver. On the first try, the ear came shooting out.

It worked! By that time, I had had about 20 years of CPR and first aid training, but had never performed the Heimlich maneuver for real.

I nicknamed my boys The Chew Crew. The irony is that they chewed everything but their food.

Mack and me
Photo courtesy of Mack's Mama

Massage—free delivery

A new acquaintance told me that she was about to pick up her very sick dog, Mack, at the veterinary hospital after the dog spent the night. I met Mack's Mama at the hospital and carried the dog to a grassy area near the parking lot.

Both Mack and his mama needed stress release. Having Mack's Mama watch me assess and massage the dog was therapeutic for her as she had been anxious about her "baby" surviving his grave illness. As I massaged Mack, I told him that it was OK to let go of his mama's worry and the anxiety of the other animals he spent the night with. Mack's shaking eased and his body relaxed into my arms. After about 20 minutes of care, Mack and his mama released their stress, and then we went our separate ways.

Sadly, Mack died a few months later.

You're not my mommy

I was walking on a windy beach where not much else could be heard besides the ocean and the wind. I did hear something else, though, something unintelligible, but I ignored it as I passed a small dog and a medium dog with their owner. I heard the sound several more times coming from behind me and decided that it might be important. I looked back and saw a woman calling her dog that had run off. "Compass!"

It turned out that the first woman I passed with the two dogs owned only one of them. Compass (rat terrier/chihuahua) just stopped to say hi to them, as they were heading south, and then she turned north and took off in a sprint away from her owner. I was headed north, too, and watched Compass run far enough ahead to be out of sight.

The owner didn't see which way Compass ran, but I did. I figured I'd be the one to come to the rescue, but I took my time to allow Compass and I to enjoy the beach. Plus, Compass reminded me of another dog I knew, so I assumed Compass would have the same behavior of that dog which liked to run away from me.

Sure enough I gained sight of Compass, again. She was sitting and resting, waiting for someone to catch up. Figuring that Compass's eyesight wasn't 20/20, I pretended to be her owner. I knelt down, put my arms out, and said, "Come here." She sprinted up to me, ran a circle around me, and said, "You're not my mommy." I stayed still with my arms out until Compass stopped, so that I wouldn't startle her. Then I grabbed her harness and picked her up.

Compass lay in my arms, which were folded across my body. She was so tired that only her body was on my forearms; her little legs hung toward the sand. We had a nice chat and 15-minute walk back to the parking lot. For such a skittish breed/mix, Compass was completely limp in my arms.

Whenever I return a dog to its owner, I like to see how the dog behaves when the owner approaches. This gives me a sense of whether or not the dog has been abused. As we approached the parking lot, Compass started shaking. *Uh oh*. The owner and Compass had a very happy reunion, but she continued to shake in her owner's arms. I decided it was because Compass was adopted from a shelter at six months old and was probably abused by the previous owner —perhaps before and after running off.

I gave Compass's current owner the all-clear.

Dogs aren't yard art

Somehow, in one neighborhood where I lived, I had the bad luck of a series of three crappy renters in the house next-door to me. Unfortunately, for the seven years I lived in that neighborhood, it became predictable that a renter would move in and then a short time later adopt a dog. Just as predictably, the owners would neglect the dog. What is one thing neglected dogs do? Bark incessantly. Ugh.

The first renter tied the dog up to a tree in the front yard and left it there all day while the couple were at work. I told the couple that I felt sorry for their dog. They said, "But, we <u>have</u> to work." *Yes, but you don't <u>have</u> to own a dog.* When they came home from work, they untied the dog from the tree and brought it into the house and probably told it to lie down. Poor thing. ZERO EXERCISE. Do you know what that does to the psyche of a dog? And that dog was a husky, a breed that needs a lot of exercise, which is why so many huskies are escape artists.

I asked the owners if it would be OK for me to go onto their property and pet the dog while they were at work. They said yes. I made each Wednesday, my bicycling day, the day when I would pet the dog. I would stop on my way back from my bike ride to pet the dog, which went nuts when I rode up. I gave the dog a five-minute rub down and then went back home. I am sure that the dog looked forward to Wednesdays. On a rare occasion, I was pressed for time and rode by without stopping. "I'm sorry. I'm sorry I can't stop."

When the couple were preparing to move, they told me that their new home had a fenced-in backyard. I was so relieved to hear that the dog would finally get some exercise.

Please don't spray me

I was riding my bicycle on a country road when I saw a skunk at one side. I stopped, because it looked like it was struggling. It looked like it had been hit. The skunk couldn't use its back legs and it was trying to get out of the road and up the embankment, maybe into one of the holes.

I don't know what a skunk's natural predators are, but where I live there are *many* turkey vultures. I knew I had to help it, even though it might not have been able to hunt or forage again.

Since I wasn't sure if it would bite me, I grabbed two sticks and put one underneath each of the skunk's underarms and started pulling the animal up the dirt.

"Which hole are you headed for?" I asked the skunk. Maybe I should have asked in French (Pepé Le Pew).

I stood to the side of the skunk, because I didn't want it to spray me. *Can it still spray me? Is spraying voluntary, involuntary, both, part of the autonomic nervous system? You know how a man who can't use his legs can still get excited? You know what I mean? His pee pee isn't controlled by the peripheral nervous system and therefore can still function.* This is what I wondered about the skunk.

I finished pulling the skunk to the hole that I thought it lived in and then I took off on my bike. On my way back, I didn't see the skunk. I hoped that it finished its journey to safety.

It's only deadly

I was walking on the beach in Lanikai, Oahu, Hawaii, which I had to myself for a while. Then I saw a woman walking toward me with her dog off the leash. She was freaking out. When the woman approached me I asked her what was wrong. In utter hysteria, she told me that the dead fish in her dog's mouth was poisonous. *That's all?* The dog looked up at me as it wagged its tail, proud of its find. *This will be easy.*

At the time I still had my dogs, Tommy and Cammy, who loved playing ball. After Tommy would return a ball, he would not put it down for me to throw. He wanted me to take it from his mouth and made it difficult for me to do so. That was part of the game for Tommy. To get the ball out of the grips of his strong jaws, I would stand on his left side facing in the same direction as he. I would place my right hand on top of Tommy's nose with my thumb on one side of his upper jaw and my other fingers on the other side of his upper jaw. With my fingers on the right side of his jaw, I would push his upper lip down and tuck it under his upper molars so that it would feel like he was biting his lip. In two quick motions I would make Tommy bite his lip and then push his lower jaw down. The ball would pop right out.

I did the same thing with the dog carrying the fish. I wasn't worried about the dog hurting me. The dog was a typically sweet golden retriever. Lip bite. Lower jaw down. Pop. Out came the fish. The dog was satisfied with leaving the fish on the beach. I guess the dog had had its fill; the dog and its owner walked on.

Echo, echo, echo

I was sitting with three acquaintances who were with their chihuahua/rat terrier dog. Even though I didn't know the dog well, and the owners weren't acting as though anything were amiss, I thought that the dog was acting strangely.

I called the dog over to me, picked it up, and asked it what was wrong. It looked at me with big eyes as if to say, "Figure it out, because those numbskulls never will." With the dog sitting on my lap and looking up at me, I put my hands close to the dog's head. Since it put its head down, I knew that I had started at the right place. I put my hands down, and the dog lifted its head up. Then I put my right hand by the left side of the dogs head and the dog put its head down. I did the same with the other side, but the dog didn't move its head. I figured the left ear was the issue.

I gently rubbed the dog's right ear, which it enjoyed as most dogs do. I touched the dog's left ear gently and the dog flinched. Even though I looked in the dog's ear and didn't see anything, I told the owners, "The dog has a foxtail in its ear." "Oh, great," was their response.

Considering this situation an emergency, the owners took the dog to the vet and then told me after, "You were wrong. There wasn't a foxtail. There were <u>two</u> foxtails." Oh, I love being right. One of my three acquaintances said, "You're so astute!" That's a good word.

Sssssnake!

When I lived in San Diego I took my dogs to the park, daily, to run, explore, and play ball. They, too, ran, explored, and played ball. Ha. The park had an upper level with a small field and playground, a lower level back off the street with a three-diamond baseball park, and a farther back area that was a hiking trail.

On this particular day, I had my boys on leash for a hike. As soon as we walked into the canyon and amongst the trees, I saw a snake. I was surprised that my boys passed it without flinching. They were quite the hunters, but I guess somewhere along their lives they learned not to challenge a snake.

The snake was caught in erosion control cloth, which is like a canvas material, mesh. One manufacturer advertises that their cloth is biodegradable. That's good news. The snake didn't have time to wait for the cloth to degrade, though.

I walked back to my truck to get scissors out of my first aid kit. Fortunately, there was a man and his son at the park whom I asked for help. We all walked back to the trail. The child held onto the boys' leashes, the man held the snake (a garter), and I cut. I was grateful to have help, because I'm squeamish when it comes to knew tactile sensations. Also, if I suddenly became scared, then my boys would have killed the snake. After we freed the snake, the man moved it off trail and away from cloth. The snake slithered happily ever after.

Another time I was at that park, next to a baseball diamond, I saw a boa constrictor sunbathing at the base of a hill by the diamond! Yikes! My boys and I were the only ones there. Was the boa someone's pet that was loose?! It reminded me of the time when I was walking past the pool at the apartment complex where I was living and I saw someone's boa taking a dip in the pool—the *whole* length of the pool.

I wanted the boa at the park to enjoy its freedom for ever after. I also worried that the next person who saw the snake would be scared and kill it. I decided to leave it be and not call animal control.

Chipped, but not forgotten

On occasion Becca* hires me to watch her two dachshunds at her house when she is out of town. I look forward to spending time with those dogs, because they remind me of the dachshund I had when I was a child.

One day when I was in the front yard, I saw a little dog walking up and down the sidewalk. I looked all around and found that there was no one claiming the dog. I grabbed a leash and put it around the friendly dog and let it lead me around the neighborhood, hoping that it would take me to where it lived. The dog went up the steps of one house and sniffed around. Even though I had a vibe that the dog didn't live there, I knocked on the door, but no one answered. I took the dog back to Becca's house, offered it food and water, and then developed another plan.

That night I spoke with Becca about the dog and asked if it could stay in the house for a couple of days while I tracked down the owner. She said OK—two days only. Becca's dogs were happy to have a guest.

The next day, I called animal control and described the dog I found and gave my contact information. There was no similar dog reported lost. Then I walked the dog to the vet and asked to have it scanned for a chip. A chip was found and the vet's secretary called the owner whose number was disconnected. I was given the owner's name, but not her phone number, which was fine because I can track down anyone.

I found an address and another phone number for the owner, who lived in Arizona! I wondered how the dog made it to California's central coast. Maybe the owner was visiting the area. I called the woman's number and left a message.

With two days having passed without connecting the dog with its owner, I called animal control to have the dog picked up at Becca's request. I cried as I watched the dog being driven away. It doesn't take long for me to bond with a dog.

Several months later I received a call from a distraught woman, who said that she heard my message about the lost dog. It was her dog and she wanted to be reunited with it! The poor woman told me her sob story, which included being homeless and having had a broken phone. She didn't say how the dog ended up in California.

I told the woman about my two days with the dog and that I had to let animal control take it. Of course she hoped I still had the dog. The best I could help the woman, at that point, was to give her animal control's phone number. Maybe they still had the dog. She thanked me and ended the conversation. I never heard from the woman, again, and doubted that she was reconnected with her dog. The good news is that the shelters in San Luis Obispo County have a high adoption, low kill rate.

The great escape

One evening I was driving down a four-lane road where there were businesses on either side. Fortunately, there weren't a lot of cars when I saw a dog running in the middle of the street and then standing in the middle. I was in the right lane noticing a bicyclist to the right waving the dog over to him. I figured that he was either trying to help the dog or he was a bad owner.

I slowed and rolled my window down and yelled, "Is that your dog?" The bicyclist said no. I pulled over, grabbed the leash that I keep in my car for just such an emergency, and headed toward the dog. The bicyclist rode off. Another driver, a man, pulled over, and then a woman stopped in the middle of the road and grabbed the dog. I walked up and put a leash on the dog and led it to the sidewalk.

Three of us Good Samaritans chatted, connecting over our rescue of the night. Bonding with strangers is an important benefit of coming to the rescue, which connects you with people you may not have spoken to otherwise. Even in this situation I can attest to that. I could tell that the man and woman engaged in smoking—something I detest. Since I stay far away from smokers, even when they're not smoking, because they always smell like an ash tray, I would not have spoken with these two beautiful souls and discovered our mutual love for dogs. Every Good Samaritan act is a lesson.

The dog was in good shape, healthy, happy, well-mannered, and precious. The man called the number on the dog's tag and told the owner that we had his dog and where we were. The owner said, "You have my dog?!" Ugh. Did I say that some people shouldn't own dogs? The owner didn't even know that his dog had left the yard, which was a couple of miles away from where we were.

The woman took off, and the man and I waited for the owner to arrive. The dog looked like a yellow lab mix, until I saw its eyes—husky! Hmm. The puzzle was coming together.

When the owner pulled up, it was time for me to decide whether or not the dog escaped a bad situation or just needed more freedom. Fortunately, it was the latter. The owner and dog had a nice reunion and it was obvious that the dog was very well-trained. I asked, "Is your dog part husky?" He said, "She's husky and basenji." I said, "Oh, that explains a lot. Huskies are escape artists."

The man and I said goodbye to the owner and dog and then walked back to our cars. I said, "Huskies are escape artists. I think it's because they're so close to their wolf ancestors." He added, "Pit bulls are escape artists, too." I replied, "I didn't know that." We parted ways.

Who put that there?

I was walking in front of a building when something flashed across my sightline. And then I heard WHAM! A small bird flew into the building's front window. The poor thing fell to the ground and then just lay there, surely seeing stars. I knelt down and did my best to assess it. The bird was able to right itself and then walked only as well as a drunken sailor.

There was a man getting out of his car, nearby, so I asked him to help. It turned that he was quite the animal whisperer having grown up with all kinds of critters. The man picked up the bird and petted it and talked to it. The bird melted into him and nuzzled his neck. After a few minutes, the bird flew off! It's amazing how healing love is.

CHAPTER 2

CARS

I bought my first car when I was 15 years old and ever since I have carried flares. I have stopped for *many* car crashes and offered flares and other types of help. My senior year in high school I became a gear head. I was the only girl in auto shop and ended the year receiving the senior academic award for industrial technology. I was the one honored out of all the seniors in auto shop, wood shop, and drafting. My knowledge about cars has led me to go with friends *many* times to speak with a mechanic.

I have also pushed *many* disabled vehicles, sometimes using my truck—as evidenced by my mangled front license plate—sometimes on foot, and sometimes on roller skates! This aid seems less about being a Good Samaritan and more about karma and reciprocation. I have had my car pushed *many* times.

Not a tempting teeter totter

When I was on a road trip, I took California's Highway 1 south back to Paso Robles. As I turned onto the highway I jokingly asked myself: *Who is driving over the cliff* [near Big Sur] *today?* I had heard of multiple fatalities leading up to my drive. Sure enough, I passed a large tow truck with a huge crane pulling up another vehicle. *Huh. What do you know?*

Not enough. That was just the start of my premonition manifesting. In San Luis Obispo County, I turned left onto Highway 46. There are a couple of lookout points at the summit, which offer a beautiful view of Morro Bay. I drove by one pullout where a car was half-way over the edge of a lookout. People were standing by the car. As I continued driving, I was deciding whether or not I was needed. I decided yes and flipped a U-ey. There was a 4-door compact teetering on the edge between flat ground and a long, steep drop to ranch land.

In the car there had been a young Mexican couple, his mother, and two young children. The man stopped at the edge and exited his vehicle to take a picture. He didn't engage the emergency brake and the automatic transmission car wasn't completely placed in park. [Note: Don't park facing a cliff. Parallel park.] As the car started rolling toward the edge, the man screamed and chased the car and jumped into the car and tried to stop it. The wife got out OK. A Black woman perched on a large nearby boulder (eight feet high) jumped off and pulled the two kids out. Another woman pulled the old woman out, who was caught up in her seat belt. Everyone was pulled out in time and the car was stopped right at the edge, pointing toward ranch land.

As I implied, I didn't see it happen; I was briefed. I showed up after the drama. The Black woman said, "I don't know how I jumped off that boulder without hurting myself." *You're youthful, clearly athletic, and Black.* The next task was to pull the car back onto flat land. I have kept a tow strap in my vehicle ever since I started owning trucks. This was to be the first time I ever used it. Unfortunately, I knew that my 2WD Toyota Tacoma wouldn't have enough torque to pull the car back over the edge. Another local, a cowboy, stopped with his large 4 x 4 truck—a common sight where I live. We hooked my tow strap to the cowboy's truck and the stranded vehicle, and I signaled both drivers. We had the Mexican man get in his vehicle so that he could punch it the same time the cowboy punched it. On the second try, the car was pulled back. We all cheered. The cowboy disconnected the tow strap and went on his way. No drama. Stop to help out and then go on with your day, very typical of residents where I live. I love that.

The last step was consoling the driver. Meanwhile, his family were in another onlooker's vehicle trying to calm down. The driver was crying, "I could have killed my whole family! I could have lost my whole family!" One of the ladies who helped out was a therapist. The three of us ladies went into counseling mode and comforted the man for about an hour after the ordeal ended. Since the car checked out fine, the Mexican family were able to continue home to Fresno. We recommended that they stop in downtown Paso Robles to let the kids play on the playground and allow the whole family to decompress and drive home with less stress.

Shoulda bought a Toyota—wait, you did

I was driving on the freeway and saw a Toyota Camry disabled on the side of the road. The hood was up and steam was billowing. I was pretty sure the steam was steam, but I pulled over in case it was smoke.

I talked with the man, who was happy to have moral support. The steam was caused by coolant being sprayed all over the engine. I had never seen anything like it before. I didn't see any busted hoses, either. He said that his car was over-heating and that he pulled over when he saw steam. I told the man that his thermostat probably busted. It was difficult to see from where the coolant spray originated since it was all over, as though someone turned a garden hose on the engine.

Since the man said a tow truck was on the way, I took off after a few minutes.

Stuck in limb-o

I was walking in a store parking lot where I stopped to say hi to a former client and her teenage daughter. After talking for a couple of minutes, we noticed that an elderly woman was standing by the driver's door of her car, distressed. I asked the woman if she were OK. She said that she locked her keys in the car. The three of us offered to help. I thought that we had a good chance of helping, because the window was partly down. I knew, though, neither my client nor I could fit our arms in. My client's daughter, a tall, thin, cross-country runner could fit her arm in. The daughter did and unlocked the door. But, the teenager couldn't get her forearm back out. I assessed the situation and noticed that her hand was in a fist. I told the teenager to relax her hand. She did, and her forearm came right out.

When we tighten a muscle, the belly of the muscle bulks. The forearm went in the window relaxed, but was tense when the teenager tried to pull it out.

This was one of those occasions when I'm excited to notice yet another way I'm able to use my knowledge of the body. I can't think of any knowledge more important to have.

I know that we could have just opened the door and rolled down the window farther, but what fun is that?

Hot! Hot!

I was driving on the freeway in a rural area where there were two lanes in each direction with a concrete and grass median. I was heading north and seeing that the other side had a crash with traffic backed up for miles. About three miles north of the crash I came upon a collision on my side, one car pulled over to the right and one half-way in the fast lane & half-way on the median. I pulled over behind the car on the median and parked in the grass.

I asked the driver by me if he were OK. He said yes. I yelled the same to the other driver, and she said yes. They both told me they called 911. So, it was time for me to play traffic cop. I grabbed a flare, lit it, and started walking south along the median motioning for cars to slow down and to drive in the right lane. The drivers stopped on the southbound side were watching me.

For even more of a visual, you need to know how I was dressed. I was wearing a beautiful red dress that I was rockin' and tennis shoes for comfort and practicality during my three-hour drive. It seemed like the show I was putting on was going to cause a third crash. Men were rubbernecking, truckers were waving and honking their horns— lots of cat calling. I enjoyed it.

When I set my ego aside for a moment, I realized that the embers that were dropping from the flare could start the weeds ablaze. So, I held the flare, still in my left hand, farther away from me so that it was over the asphalt instead of weeds. I noticed that my left foot was getting hot, but I ignored it because I needed to stay focused. *Maybe you should look down. It could be important.* I looked down and saw that my left shoe was smoldering! An ember fell on my shoe. I did a Mexican hat dance. *Hot! Hot! Hot!* I ripped off my shoe, saw that my sock was smoldering, ripped off my sock, and saw that my foot at the base of my toes was red but OK. I looked up and laughed at the reaction of the people watching my show.

After about 10 minutes of excitement, I was nearing the end of the flare and my pain tolerance when I saw a fire truck coming. I placed the flare on the asphalt and put my foot part-way into my hot shoe and hobbled back to my car, carrying my sock.

It is funny to think about what each passerby saw. The people on the southbound side saw everything. The stranded drivers on the northbound side probably watched me through their rear-view mirrors and wondered: *What is she doing?* Some of the northbound drivers saw this sexy girl walking with a lit flare in total control of traffic; the next set saw a girl doing a Mexican hat dance; the final set saw me hobbling back to my car.

Light as a feather, stiff as a ladder

I was driving in the middle lane on a freeway in a rental car; not too many people were out. Ahead of me I saw a pick-up truck with an aluminum ladder in the back. I started imagining air catching the untethered ladder and the ladder flying out of the truck toward me. Not wanting to pay extra for my car rental, I slowed and greatly increased my distance from the truck.

Just then—sure enough—the ladder flew out of the truck. It seemed to go airborne in slow motion and then gradually float in steps to the ground, landing right in front of where I stopped. I weighed my options of 1) remaining stopped to protect others from hitting the ladder and 2) being rear-ended. I motioned the best I could to alert the other drivers.

With a semi quickly approaching, I took off into the fast lane and wished the other drivers good luck. I saw people come to an abrupt stop, but that's all I know. I wouldn't at all be surprised if there were a crash.

Cable or noose

I ran into a friend Josh* who was upset about his car being in the shop. I asked him what happened. He said that he needed a new clutch, something that he couldn't afford.

I said, "OK. Slow down. Tell me what happened."

He said, "I was driving [my old car] and when I went to shift again I pressed the clutch pedal and the pedal went right to the floor. There was no resistance."

"It sounds like your clutch cable broke. You don't need a new clutch. This is what we're going to do. We'll go to Kragen's, we'll buy a new cable which will cost about $20, and then we'll take it to the mechanic and tell him to install it."

"OK."

I drove Josh to Kragen's, he bought the cable, and I drove him to the mechanic. "Let me do all the talking," I told Josh.

Standing in the mechanic's shop, I held the clutch cable behind my back and asked the mechanic what was wrong with the car. Of course I played it like I didn't know anything about cars.

"The clutch went out. I'm gonna have to put a new one in," the mechanic proclaimed.

"I see." Then like a magician pulling a rabbit out of a hat, I displayed the clutch cable. "We'd like you to install the clutch cable and do no other work. Josh will be back in an hour to pick up his car. Thank you." Before I walked away I gave the mechanic a shame-on-you look.

I left Josh at the shop. When I saw him the next day he was elated. "Thank you thank you thank you. My car is running great again, and it didn't cost much. I owe you lunch."

Josh never did take me out to lunch. It's OK. I know what it's like to be broke.

Yo hablo Español, a veces

I lived in San Diego, California, from December 1992 to February 2004. I unaffectionately state that I did time in San Diego—11 years. I didn't like living there, but that's another story for another book.

Living in a big city there is plenty of opportunity to come to someone's rescue, especially on the freeway. One night that I was driving on freeway 805, I was the second person to stop for a crash in the slow lane before emergency personnel arrived. I didn't see what happened. I did see the potential impending doom, though. A Mexican man's compact car looked like it had been in a trash compactor. The back of his car was smashed accordion style all the way up to the front seats and the car was facing south on the northbound side of the freeway.

The man who arrived before me was holding the driver's head still and straight until EMT arrived with a C (cervical [spine]) collar. Distressed, the Mexican man said, "Yo quiero a llamar por teléfono mi hija." I want to call my daughter. I understood that. Then he kept pointing to his reading glasses on the floor. I was so amped from adrenaline that I couldn't remember how to say glasses— anteojos. The Mexican man wanted his glasses so that he could look up his daughter's phone number and then give it to us so that we could call her. This was before cell phones. I was frustrated that I couldn't remember anteojos. The man who was helping didn't speak Spanish. "After this is over, I'm going to sign up for a Spanish class." I said, "And I'm going to study my Spanish-English dictionary."

It was pretty scary standing in a freeway lane at night, hoping no one would barrel into us. Finally, police and EMT arrived, and the two of us Good Samaritans were able to leave. I don't remember anything about another car involved, but obviously there was one.

Nothing to see here

In Lake Tahoe, I was driving from a wedding reception to the wedding party's next festivity when I saw a disabled vehicle on the right side of the boulevard. There was no shoulder or even a bike lane, so I needed to get the driver and his car off the street. I pulled up behind him and asked if I could help. The driver said yes. We agreed that I would use my truck to push him to the next driveway and parking lot.

Meanwhile, one-by-one, wedding guests recognized my truck and thought that *I* was the one needing help. They didn't see that I was pushing a car. So, they slowed down and asked if I needed help. I waved each by; they were blocking the other lane and potentially getting in my way. One even started pulling in front of the car I was pushing. I yelled, "No! Go!"

I was able to get the car into the parking lot, and then I left.

CHAPTER 3

ADULTS

Even though I have a degree in physical education and have had a career in health and fitness, I still stand in wonderment how I know what to do when someone is in acute health crisis. I've never considered first aid my strong point, although I have always been so good at CPR I could teach it. I guess one of the reasons why I haven't considered myself good at first aid is because it requires immediate action. I would prefer to ponder, read, and analyze before taking action. "Let's talk about it." Ha. How do I know what to do? I know a lot about the body—I'm a physiology junky—but many occasions are beyond my scope of training. I can't help but wonder if during a medical crisis I channel my great-grandfather who was a doctor.

Also, I have my cousin Jade* in my head when I am aiding someone. Jade is a retired emergency room physician. Many years ago I told her that I considered becoming a doctor, but that I would not have made a good emergency room physician because I would rather ponder than act fast. She said, "Yes, you would." That simple response made a huge impact on me and fueled my confidence in knowing what to do when I'm put on the spot.

In this and other chapters you'll read door knocking stories. I started door knocking when I was five years old, selling Girl Scout cookies. When I was a little older I sold flowers that I picked from neighbors' yards. One time a neighbor asked, "Jeanne, did you pick that from my yard?"

I said, "No." A lie. I'm sure my neighbor knew I lied, but she bought the flower anyway. I felt so bad I took the experience as a lesson never to lie to a customer again—and I haven't. I also door knocked to drum up other business like house and dog sitting.

After I started my business in 1992, I continued door knocking and still do it, because it's what I know. Plus, selling my services and books in person is my strength, as opposed to earning money online. You can imagine that after a lifetime of door knocking I can write a book on it—two books: one about how to door knock effectively and safely, and one about the people I meet. People show their true colors when a door knocker arrives at their homes. So much so, I thought about offering a service of door knocking in a neighborhood where someone is thinking about buying a home. I could tell the potential home owner where the meth lab is, the wife beater, the dog that barks incessantly, the preacher, the gossip—and that's just one house! Ha!

Granny, can you hear me?

When I was door knocking selling my books, an older gentleman opened the door and was quite friendly. He declined to buy one of my books, because he didn't have time to read. Caring for his wife, who had dementia and no longer spoke, was a continuous effort.

The man invited me into his house to meet his wife, because she didn't get out much and could use a friendly face. For other reasons including keeping myself safe, I rarely accept an invitation into someone's home. How dangerous can a home of two elderly people be? I'll tell you. Sometimes there is an adult child who still lives at home and, normally, has issues. I looked past the man and didn't see a third person in the house, so I accepted the invitation.

The woman was sitting in a chair in the living room just off the front entrance. While the man was standing behind me, I kneeled beside her and said hello and introduced myself. I put my hand on her forearm, dropped my head, closed my eyes, and gave her my energy. After a few minutes, I opened myself up to receive a message from her. It was something to the effect: "Get me out of here."

I opened my eyes, saw that her eyes were still closed, and then did a double take to my right. Standing in the kitchen watching me was . . . a man in his forties. *Oh, great.* After the younger man saw me, he walked away. The older man said to me, "That's my son. He has issues." *Aw, fuck. And that's why the woman has checked out.* Then, I checked out. "OK, I have to go. Nice meeting you. Thank you for inviting me in." I left dust behind me like you would see in a cartoon.

Dried out

I walked into a night club that had a band playing and people sitting at tables and at the bar. There was a little bit of room in front of the stage for dancing. After I looked around, I saw someone I knew and I walked across the club to say hi. After a few minutes, I walked back toward the front of the club, passing the stage again. The bar had leather, S-shaped bar seats with a low back. One end of the bar was right by the stage. There was an elderly woman sitting at the end of the bar with her seat turned sideways facing the band. Her husband was turned the same way seated behind her. After I passed the stage and saw the elderly woman, I knew something wasn't right. I stopped and stood right in front of her. The woman's husband had his hands on her shoulders; she kept listing left and he kept straightening her. I said to the woman, "Had a little too much vino?" She didn't respond. Then, I recognized the woman's eyes—I saw right through them: dementia. I stayed in front of her, knowing that she was about to have a medical emergency. Keep in mind the band was still playing, and I was the only one who knew that something bad was going to happen. And it did. The elderly woman slithered out of the chair, and I caught her. I pulled her away from the chair, where her feet were caught within the foot rest, and then laid her on her back on the floor right in front of the stage. The full house looked on, and the band continued to play. At the end of the song, the band finally paused, and I assessed the woman who had fainted but remained conscious. Trumping my skills, two paramedics in the audience took over, and someone else called an ambulance. I whispered to the husband, "Does your wife have dementia?" He said, "Yes."

I found out later that the woman fainted because she was dehydrated, a common symptom of people with dementia because they forget to drink water and their caregivers overlook this need. Oh, minor detail, the woman was drinking alcohol—a diuretic. Why people let those with dementia drink alcohol is beyond me. Stupid! Alcohol kills brain cells.

Whale of a slip

When I was in junior high, my family and I were in San Diego visiting my grandfather whom I absolutely adored. He was tall (you'd never guess we were related) with a medium build and fair skin akin to his Canadian pedigree. When we went on walks I wore my roller skates to keep up with him.

One day we were at Sea World—a place I came to despise because of their captivity of orcas. Anyway, my immature mind wasn't quite there, yet, and I enjoyed the killer whale show. Although we were seated high enough not to get wet, the cement steps were damp.

After the show, my grandfather and I walked side-by-side down the steps. He slipped, and I caught him. Although my grandfather was in his early eighties at the time and in good shape, he lost is balance. He said, "You're strong." My grandfather was grateful that I was there for him and he boasted for days about my strength. I was filled to the rim with self-esteem and his love. All of my years of playing on the bars and playing sports paid off.

My grandfather's gratitude and how it made me feel is evidence of how the littlest comment, good or bad, can make a *profound* effect on a child. So, make it good.

Don't look down

When I was in college, a bunch of us friends drove up to Lake Tahoe to snow ski. At the end of a long day of skiing, three of us girls hitched a ride on a ski lift back down the mountain. Have you ever ridden a ski lift up a mountain? Have you ever ridden a ski lift down a mountain? There's a big difference.

Riding a ski lift up a mountain, your weight is pushed back against the seat. Riding down a mountain, your weight is pushed toward the ground far, far below. It's scary. I do have a bit of fear of heights, but since I get a high off of doing what's scary, I keep the fear in check.

I was sitting on the left side of the chair, and my friend in the middle said that she was scared, really scared. My friend sitting on the right side said that she was scared, too. *Don't tell her (the friend in the middle) that! So am I, but I'm not going to tell her. That will just make her more scared.*

My friend in the middle started hyperventilating and panicking. What's worse than being on a chair lift with a measly bar in front of you? Being on a chair lift with someone who is panicking. Hyperventilation is also known as hyperoxia—too much oxygen. When we inhale we take in oxygen and other elements, and we exhale carbon dioxide and unused oxygen. Breathing in a brown paper bag is effective to treat hyperoxia, because the person has to inhale recycled air, which becomes less and less oxygen-rich.

Of course I didn't have a brown paper bag with me two miles up. So I said, "Look at me. Focus on me. Breathe with me." I had my friend's breath match mine. I breathed shallow, slowly, and held my breath intermittently. We did

this all the way down the mountain. It worked. At the
bottom, my friend said, "Thanks, Bean."

Short cut

I attended a concert at an amphitheater and then had the bright idea of driving through the pick-up area to make the quickest exit. When I was second in line to pick up my invisible friend, strange behavior came from an SUV in front of me. I saw the passenger door open and close and open and close and open and close. Because of my angle, I couldn't tell if someone were in the passenger seat or if it were the driver trying to keep the door open.

And then kerplop. A woman fell out of the passenger side of the tall vehicle and did a face plant in the decomposed granite ground. I bolted out of my car to help her. She was in her 70s and wasted. *Hey, lady! When is the party going to end? You're not in college anymore . . . and you're 70+!*

I knelt next to the lady and assessed her. She was conscious and mumbling. I said, "I'm Jeanne. I'm going to help you." I could see that her face was scratched, but she was in decent condition. "I'm going to roll you onto your back, OK?" I asked a lady nearby to help me. She did and then stepped back.

By the time I had the drunk woman on her back, I noticed that quite a crowd had gathered. I was amazed that in an emergency people just gawk, too frozen to act. I said, "Call an ambulance," forgetting that there is usually medical staff at concerts. Someone said that an EMT was on the way.

Then another woman knelt next to me and talked with the drunk woman. It turned out that they were friends. I said to this other woman, "Maxine*!" She said, "Jeanne!" Maxine is a retired physician. Trumping my expertise, I let her take over. As I was leaving, an ambulance showed up.

I was at a pizza parlor eating dinner by myself and working on my computer. The business was full of customers, and the workers were struggling to keep up. It was typical for the restaurant to make customers wait an inordinate amount of time for a meal.

One Middle Eastern-looking man was understandably very impatient, waiting for his pizza, and walked up to the counter to voice his frustration. Meanwhile, two drunk middle-aged women at a nearby table were mocking him and faulting him for being angry. About five minutes later, the man's pizza was finished and he went to his table with his pop (drink). His anger waned and he sat quietly and alone at his table, enjoying his meal. I don't know if the man noticed how the drunk women were acting, but I don't think he would have cared. He was about to find out anyway.

Ten minutes later, the women were ready to leave and made a point to go out the door by which the man was sitting. One woman walked all the way out, and the other stopped and spewed vulgarities at the man. The woman's behavior escalated while the man ignored her. *Doesn't she realize he's seen much worse where he's from? Hasn't she ever seen video of a convenience store owner grabbing a machete and running after an armed robber?*

This whole time I kept looking around the restaurant. *Doesn't anyone else see what's happening? Why is the staff so clueless?* Then, the woman picked up the man's drink and was posed to throw it in his face. *Alright. No more.* I walked over and calmly stood near the woman, who continued stating mean remarks. I gradually put my body between the table and the woman. I said, "It's over." I put two fingers on her wrist near the drink and slowly and gently started pushing down. I quietly said, "It's over. It's OK. It's over. It's time to go. It's over." The woman put the drink down, let go of it, and started backing up. I further wedged myself between the table and herself and herded her toward the door. "It's OK. It's over. Time to go." I kept my energy very calm.

The woman walked out. When I turned around, there was a huge man looking down at me. He said, "I had your back."

"Thank you," I replied.

"I used to be a bouncer."

"Oh, so you've dealt with that plenty."

"Yeah."

I looked at the man eating his pizza, but he did not make eye contact with me or say anything. I went back to my table. I'll let you use your imagination as to what he was thinking about the drunk woman and my rescue.

To whom am I speaking?

When I was in a park I had to get away from a man who was walking toward me to do his usual stalking of women —especially me. Fucking predators. I went up to a man sitting at a table and asked if I could sit with him. Let's call this man Tim*. Tim said, "Yes." I pretended like we knew each other so stalker dude would walk away. He did. Little did I know I was sitting with a man who had a different mental illness. He seemed a little off, but I didn't think too much of it. After about 30 minutes I thanked him for letting me sit with him and then I took off.

A month later, I was about to get in my car across the street from the same park when I sensed a commotion. Tim was walking down the middle of the street yelling. People were looking at him from all angles. Then, my mind flashed to the other times I saw him in the park in the last few weeks and the people he seemed to know. *Oh. He's part of that group.* I assumed he lived in a group home for people who are a little off.

"Tim," I called. He walked over to me. I opened my car door to use as a buffer just in case. "What's going on?"

Tim said, "My brother fought for our country. What have people done for him? He fought for our country."

This dialogue sounded familiar. I remembered Tim saying the same thing when I sat with him, but this time he was highly agitated. It doesn't really matter what else he said while standing in front of me. What matters is that Tim repeated the same four sentences. His brain was stuck.

I kept my energy calm and spoke to Tim like a therapist, validating his comments. Out of the corner of my eye, I saw someone across the street waving me over to get away from Tim. I nonchalantly nodded to show I was OK.

After a few rounds on repeat, I asked, "Tim, do you remember when I met you in the park? I'm Jeanne. You let me sit at your table."

He said, "That was you?"

"Yes."

Tim thought about it and softened his tone, but continued the broken record.

I said, "I heard what you have to say. I appreciate what your brother did for our country. I have to go now. I'm going to get in my car and shut the door. Bye." I sat in my car and shut the door. Tim walked off a little calmer than a few minutes prior, but unfortunately still stuck. Poor guy. I think he was schizophrenic off his meds.

After Tim walked off, I rolled down my window to talk with two men who were standing by a tree in front of my truck. I had barely noticed them.

They said, "We had your back."

I said, "Aw, thank you. Poor guy."

"You handled that great."

"I've had a lot of experience counseling, but I've never encountered someone like that before."

"You did everything perfectly."

"Thanks. See ya'."

I firmly believe those two men had military or law enforcement experience. I don't know much about either, but their training must include how to handle an escalated situation between two people. I was so impressed that they didn't jump right in and pick a fight or act like tough guys otherwise. They noticed that I was doing well, but they stood by just in case. I can't give them enough praise for their tactic. I should even praise them for their acting performance. They stood by the tree as though they were interested in the tree. Tim never noticed them.

National Alliance on Mental Illness, www.nami.org, provides an information card that looks like a business card. It is titled Communicating with Someone who has a Psychiatric Illness; the card contains the following:

Proceed to interact as you:
1. be [sic] calm and give firm, clear instructions;
2. assess the situation for safety;
3. maintain appropriate space between you and the person;
4. respond to apparent feelings;
5. respond to delusions and hallucinations by talking about the person's feelings rather than what he is saying;
6. be [sic] helpful, encouraging, and supportive.

Avoid:
1. reinforcing behavior related to the person's illness;
2. staring at the person, this may be interpreted as a threat;
3. confusing the person;
4. giving multiple choices, this increases confusion;
5. whispering, yelling, ridiculing, deceiving or touching. This may cause more fear and lead to violence.

Someone with a psychiatric illness might:	So you need to:
Have trouble with reality.	Be simple, truthful
Be fearful.	Stay calm
Be insecure.	Be accepting
Have trouble concentrating.	Be brief, repeat
Be overstimulated.	Limit input
Easily become agitated.	Recognize agitation
Have poor judgment.	Not expect rational discussion
Be preoccupied.	Get attention first
Be withdrawn.	Initiate relevant conversation
Have changing emotions.	Disregard
Have changing plans.	Keep to one plan
Have little empathy for you.	Recognize as a symptom
Believe delusions.	Ignore, don't argue
Have low self-esteem and motivation.	Stay positive

So much for the certification

I was in a library working on my computer, aware that the library was about to close. As I was ending the programs on my computer, I could hear over my music, "Sir, are you OK? Sir, are you OK? Sir." I finished packing up and thought I better check out the scene, considering that there are a lot of druggies and homeless people and homeless druggies who hang out in the library.

I walked around a book shelf and saw a man lying on the floor face down and a librarian standing over him. "Did you check for a pulse?" I asked. "No. Another librarian is calling 911," she said. I gently kicked the man's feet, but he didn't move. I knelt by him and nudged him, but he was unresponsive and unconscious. I spoke to the man. Nothing. I felt for a pulse at his wrist and neck. Nothing. I noticed that the man's socks were stuffed with paraphernalia. For drugs? I put my hand near his nose to feel for a breath. I couldn't feel anything. So, I decided it was time to flip the man over. As I moved him, he moved on his own accord a little, but he was still out cold. Since the man moved, I had enough information to know that he was breathing and had a pulse.

I stood up and saw EMT walk in. I walked back to my table to grab my stuff and leave. The librarian who called 911 walked toward the man on the floor and then yelled to me, "The library's closed!"

I said, "I know. I was helping the man." I was furious. *That's the thanks I get for helping?!* The librarian who watched everything I did should have spoken up, but didn't.

"We don't need your help. We're trained in CPR," the annoying librarian continued.

"If you were trained in CPR, then why weren't you going through the CPR steps? You obviously aren't any good at it."

"The library's closed."

Oh, I was about to lose it. "I know. That's why I'm leaving!" To make matters worse, a third librarian ushered me out as though I were a liability. I was over the top insulted. No one ever thanked me for helping, not that day or any other day that I was in the library subsequently.

I think that the unconscious man was on a drug that was a depressant, which is why his pulse was too faint for me to sense. As I was LED out of the library, I saw the EMT roll the man over, and then the man sat up.

Who's the wicked one?

I was in a business hanging out when a man walked in and acted strangely. None of the workers knew what to do with him, but they realized they didn't want him there. I could tell that the man was mentally disturbed, maybe schizophrenic, so I spoke to him calmly and pretended like everything was fine.

I made good progress in keeping the man calm and shepherding him toward the door, when a woman in the store walked up between the man and me and started talking aggressively to him. *Ugh. I was making good progress.* The man became agitated and resisted leaving. Then the woman threatened to call the police, and the man conceded and left.

After the man left, the woman said to me, "I was trying to save you."

I said, "I don't need saving."

"I have mental illness in my family."

Duh.

Will the real old lady please stand up?

I saw an older woman fall in the parking lot of a bank. I assessed that she was OK and helped her to stand up. Did I simply pick up the lady? Of course not. Of course I wasn't going to make it easy for her. Of course I made the lady work for it. I made the experience a teaching moment.

I said, "I'm going to teach you how to stand up. Get onto your hands and knees. Now lift up your torso; you can hold onto my hands for balance. Now put one foot forward so that you're in a lunge position. Now stand up."

The woman stood right up. Even more valuable than doing things for others is teaching them how to help themselves.

Suicide is incredibly selfish

One day I heard in local news that a high school girl walked onto the freeway, the night before, and purposely stepped in front of a car. She was killed instantly. When I heard the driver's name my heart sank. He had been a client of mine.

The man was physically fine, but his car was badly damaged. Knowing that he had a precious soul and a big heart, I was sure he was devastated by what happened. I made it my mission to track down my client and provide comfort.

It took me a couple of weeks, but I met up with Bill*. I let him talk. I listened. I find that most people don't have anyone who will truly listen and validate their feelings. I had a lot I wanted to say but, again, most helpful is to just listen.

I did ask him to write three words:

I AM ENOUGH

And he did. And he is. And I am. And you are.

Damage control

My first and only cruise, so far, was on Holland America in the Caribbean (previous page: Panama Canal locks at sunrise). It was great! I had so much fun and made friends with the ship's security officer.

I kind of sort of went by myself. I signed up with a tour company led by a couple I knew and accompanied by four people who were in a celiac disease support group I had led.

The cruise lasted ten days. Since our group had to be on a special diet, gluten free, we were instructed by the cruise line to sit at the same three tables each night with the same tour group participants. This set-up made it easier for the waiters to keep track of us and to make sure that our meals were in fact gluten free. I thought that this request seemed reasonable. Sure, it's nice to change tables and meet others, but 1) I wanted to help the staff help me, and 2) there were plenty of other opportunities to make new friends.

The food and service were 5-star level, and I thoroughly enjoyed the royalty experience. Unfortunately, toward the end of the cruise some of the people in my group were acting like snobs and treating the waiters like shit. After a minor mistake with one dessert, the natives became restless. Some of my table mates whined about being told where to sit. Their behavior led to a crescendo of mistreating a few of the waiters. On the second-to-last day, I asked my new friend, the security officer, to pay a visit to our group that evening. He did.

When the security officer came to dinner, he discretely assessed the situation as I boasted about the food and service. After he left and I finished dinner, I went up to each of our waiters, each in tears, and did damage control.

"You are a great waiter. I appreciate you. You provide great service, and I have thoroughly enjoyed the meals. I know you're upset. My table mates are being snobs. This isn't about you. They are just being mean. I will make sure that your boss knows that you did nothing wrong."

Then, I headed to the back of the ship and thought about jumping off. I wanted to get the fuck off the boat. I felt stuck. This experience was before I knew I was an empath and well before I knew how to manage others' emotions I felt. *I'm a good swimmer. I'm sure I can make it to Florida. Cubans have.*

Later, I met up with the security officer, who asked me if I would write a letter to Holland America's corporate office to tell my side of the story. I happily did—while still on the ship—which helped me to feel better.

I don't know what ever happened to the wait staff. Probably nothing. Perhaps working with snobby elitists (is that redundant?) is just another day at the office.

Hitting the wrong note

When I was taking a voice training class at a junior college, our teacher recommended that we attend a Christmas performance where she was to lead a chorus. I attended, and so did a lot of other people, including students from my class. There were so many people that the ballroom was standing room only.

I stood off to one side in an aisle next to the wall. After about 1 1/2 hours, the show was nearing its end and so was a woman standing near me. She stood longer than her heart could handle and she fainted, falling onto a man's electric wheelchair and then the ground. People around us called 911 while I assessed the woman. Meanwhile, I had to do damage control with the man in the wheelchair who was freaking out because the woman broke the chair's joystick.

The woman remained conscious, and I determined that she didn't hurt her head or any other body part. Near me was a nurse who was in my voice class. She watched over me and had my back if I needed it.

The performance ended, an ambulance arrived, I decided that I had helped enough, and I left. A few days later when my class met, again, I spoke with the nurse about what happened. I was emotional and hard on myself, because I didn't call 911. In first aid and CPR training, it's drilled into us to call 911 as soon as it is determined that someone is in a medical crisis. I tend to get so wound up in assessing and treating people that I forget to call or tell someone to call 911. The nurse was really sweet, "Several people were calling 911 and everyone else was just standing around watching. You're the only one who did something." I still get choked up thinking about her kind words.

When we stand for a long period of time without moving, blood pools in our legs. With less blood to circulate, heart rate increases and blood pressure drops. The body is designed to faint when blood pressure drops too much, because when the body is flat it is easier for blood to return to the heart than when we are standing. In a lying position blood pressure and heart rate normalize.

Stay in your seat

When I fly commercially, as opposed to in a dream (ha), I normally sit in the back row. These seats have benefits including no one pushing or kicking me. As I was getting situated, I noticed a stewardess in a jump seat looking ill.

After the plane was at cruising altitude and I was allowed to roam, I checked on the stewardess. She was sitting across two jump seats with one leg up, icing that shin. The stewardess's face was white—you know that look when you're about to vomit. She was in a lot of pain; I believe so much so that she was nauseated. I asked the stewardess if I could help, and she said yes. I placed a towel under her knee and one on her shin to be a barrier between the ice and her skin. I asked the stewardess how long she had been icing, and she said 30 minutes. I told her to take a break for 30 minutes and then ice, again, for only ten. "Let me know if I can do anything else for you."

When I was standing over the stewardess, about to walk away, she looked up at me as though she was thinking: *Please don't leave me, my angel.* I would have stayed with her the whole flight, but I didn't ask to. I figured I would have been told no.

I never found out what happened, but I'm pretty sure the stewardess fractured her tibia (shin bone) during flight preparation. I figured that she was hit hard by a food cart. I don't know why the stewardess couldn't leave the plane, since it was still at the gate when the accident happened.

Crack!

I was playing in a co-ed softball game, in right field, when a man hit a line drive into the female second baseman's knee. I heard CRACK. The ball went right into her patella (knee cap). I knew for sure the bone was fractured. My teammate dropped to the ground and I sprinted in to help her. She was quickly taken off the field and replaced.

After the half-inning ended, I checked on my teammate in the dug out. She had a bag of ice right on her knee with her knee straight. I rolled a sweatshirt and put it under my teammate's knee to take tension off the soft tissue around the patella. Then I lightly ran one of my fingers on her skin from her lower thigh over the patella and to the top of her shin. If someone says OW with that light of a touch, the bone is usually broken. My teammate said OW. I also pulled her pant leg down and re-placed the ice. Ice shouldn't be placed directly on the skin, because the skin can be burned. Think: freezer burn.

Before we went back out in the field, I told my teammate to take the ice off her knee, because icing should be done for 10-15 minutes at a time. Icing helps to reduce swelling, but you don't want your body part so cold that circulation ceases.

When it was our turn to bat, again, I told my teammate that it was time to go to the emergency room. "I'm sure you have a simple [as opposed to compound] fracture. Ice on the way." In my many years of training it was enforced never to diagnose or render medical advice. I've always been happy to break the rules if it meant that someone would go to the doctor. My teammate went.

I didn't see my teammate for years after the accident. When I saw her, again, I didn't recognize her; she reminded me who she was. "Remember me? You helped me when I was beamed in the knee. I did fracture the bone. After I made a full recovery with no limitations, my doctor said, 'It's thanks to the proper first aid of your teammate that your knee is perfectly healthy.'"

Tongue-tied

I was staying at my friend Alice's* house for the night when she invited her friend Ron* over for me to meet. Since I was visiting from out of town, Alice thought that it would be a good opportunity for me to meet Ron with whom I had spoken on the phone twice before then.

I spoke with Ron on the phone the evening Alice invited him over. Ron said that he didn't want to come over, because he wasn't feeling well. He said that he had a really bad rash on his face from stress, so his doctor diagnosed. I coerced Ron to come over anyway.

When Ron arrived, my eyes popped out of my head. That was no rash; Ron's face and tongue were swollen and he was having difficulty swallowing. He was on the cusp of anaphylaxis—severe allergic reaction. Ron said that he had been under a lot of stress, and that his doctor confirmed the rash was from stress. After I told Ron that he should fire his doctor, I drilled Ron about what he had been eating and explained that if he were to eat the allergen one more time he might die. He said that he had been eating leftovers of a seafood meal. I gave Ron a short lesson on food allergy and told him that at any age he could develop an allergic reaction to a food. He left after an hour, and my worry elevated.

I went home the next day and worried about Ron incessantly. After a few days, I called to check in on him. He said that he was OK, but had had a rough week. Sure enough Ron consumed the allergen one more time and ended up in the emergency room where he was given epinephrine, the antidote to anaphylaxis. It turned out that his stress was also causing stomach upset for which he was taking Pepto Bismol—a lot of Pepto Bismol. The active ingredient in that medicine is bismuth subsalicylate aka salicylic acid aka aspirin. Ron had developed an aspirin allergy.

I gave Ron more information about allergy and suggested he wear a medical ID bracelet to warn emergency personnel of his allergy.

A note about stress: Stress is an umbrella term for all negative emotions, including but not limited to fear, anger, vulnerability, sadness, disgust, and jealousy. Most disease and pain has an emotion component. In a sense, Ron's doctor was right in that Ron's symptoms were caused by stress. It wasn't that simple, though. Ron's stress triggered an allergic reaction to a substance that was previously safe for him.

A note about medicine: Take away the negative emotion and the dialogue you created about an event/situation in your life, and you won't need medicine. Your body can heal itself. It's designed to heal itself! Let's say I have been having headaches that I realize are caused by fear of my boyfriend breaking up with me. I can change the internal dialogue from "I'm a terrible girlfriend" to "I am a loving girlfriend who is enough." Replaying and believing this dialogue removes the fear. Removing the fear removes the headaches. No headaches, no medicine necessary.

Real ID

When I find a lost item, I normally take it upon myself to reunite the item with its owner. I love going into amateur detective mode and figuring out who owns the item and how to reach the owner. Also, I know that the item is in good hands with me and won't be held hostage by someone else for "safe keeping."

I found a wallet in a library bathroom. I love finding wallets! It's fun to see what people carry around with them. Oh, yeah, you betcha, I look through wallets. I consider it my reward. Plus, I need evidence to figure out the owner, right? A driver's license isn't enough. Ha.

I recognized the photo on the driver's license as one of the librarians. I went up to the front desk and asked if she were available. "She went home," I was told. I didn't announce that I found someone's wallet, because I already had a reason from the CPR story not to trust some of the librarians.

My ID has my post office box as my address, but this driver's license had the librarian's physical address. I cross-checked it with a people finder's website and found that she still lives there. I delivered the wallet to her house. "I didn't even know it was missing. Thank you." Mission accomplished. And I got what I wanted out of it: a thank you . . . oh, and a journey through someone's wallet.

Hard-headed

I was playing in the Oceano (California) Dunes on quad runners (a type of ATV) with family one afternoon. Some of us, including myself, were brought out by the quad rental company, and the rest were driven by a relative named Ian*. I wasn't riding, because I had a forehead wound and therefore I couldn't wear a helmet.

At one point I was standing by Ian's truck chatting with his two kids while everyone else was out playing. A relative named Keith* drove up on a quad and stopped at the truck. He had blood dripping down his face and out of the bottom of the helmet. Keith didn't know where the blood was coming from. It turned out that he had gone down a steep slope and instead of going up the next slope, his quad came to an abrupt halt but his body kept moving. Keith slammed the front of his helmet into the handle bars.

It was a good thing (or not) Keith was wearing his helmet. When he took off his helmet, blood gushed from his forehead. I had the kids call back the rest of the family, including their dad who was an EMT. Since I didn't have my truck or hiking pack, I didn't have any first aid equipment on me. Ian came right away, and the two of us treated Keith's two-inch-long, vertical, skull-deep incision wound on his forehead. An incision wound is a cut with smooth sides, as opposed to a laceration, which has jagged edges. We stopped the bleeding, and then all of us left the dunes. I took Keith to the hospital for stitches.

I still don't know if the helmet were defective or if it were too old. Motorcycle and bicycle helmets are to be replaced every few years. Check with the manufacturer for their recommendation.

Keith healed well.

Who put that there?

I had an appointment at 12 p.m. that I was looking forward to—getting my hair cut. So, yes, a high priority the appointment was. As I was coming upon the part of a road where there was construction, I passed a car (going the other direction) that was coming to a stop in the middle of the road. I saw that it was leaking a lot of water and dropped what I thought was part of the radiator.

Help or hair? Help or hair? I really need a haircut. Dammit. Why do I always have to play savior? I flipped a U-ey. At the very least I needed to get the car part out of the road. As I picked it up and threw it onto the median, I decided that it was the dust guard, which protects the bottom of the engine. I went back into my car and drove up and parked behind the minivan that was having the problem. At the same time, a male driver pulled up alongside of the van to help.

The driver of the minivan stepped out of the car and turned out to be an elderly woman. *Dammit. I'm all in now. A senior. I love seniors. But my hair!* It turned out that the construction and uneven lanes confused the woman, and she drove over the new median, breaking the dust guard and I think a radiator hose. I asked if she were OK, while I looked in the car and saw that the passenger air bag deployed. I couldn't see if the driver's bag deployed. Then my eyes went wide. I looked closer at the woman and saw that her left forearm was bleeding profusely and had two huge lumps. *Now I'm really all-in.*

I told the man to call 911. He gave me a blank stare. Then I told him to take the woman to the sidewalk to get her out of the street. The man didn't do that either. *Must I do everything?* I called 911 while walking the woman across the street.

With ambulance on the way, I grabbed my first aid kit and started treating the woman's forearm wound and determining the source of the bleeding. I found a small cut, which was compounded by a blood thinner, hence the huge bumps (impact injuries). A cut can also result from an impact, especially if one's skin is as thin as this woman's was, typical of seniors. I still don't know how she injured her forearm.

I also determined that the woman, probably in her 80s, had mild dementia. Yes, she shouldn't have been driving. When emergency personnel showed up, I had the man brief the cops, since he was the only one who saw what happened, and I briefed the paramedics. Deciding that the woman was in good hands and would probably be fine, I took off.

The woman was calm, not in pain, and seemed emotionally unaffected by the incident. A couple days later I decided that as far as emergency situations there is a difference between seniors with dementia and seniors cognitively healthy. I have observed that seniors with dementia are totally unfazed by an emergency, whereas other seniors' minds race a million miles an hour. How will I get home? Is my car totaled? Will insurance cover the damages? Will I lose my license? Am I going to die?

The day after the crash I noticed that someone posted a story on social media about the incident. It was pretty amusing to see all of the erroneous assumptions people made. They must be professional journalists! One person even wrote about the new median: "Who puts a median in the middle of the road?" I responded, "Where else would a median go?" Moron.

As for the irony of this story, the construction was due to a new memory care facility being built. As for people acting fast when they smell a lawsuit, the road was magically finished two days after the crash. You can see in the picture that the street looks perfectly fine. I took the photograph two days after the crash.

Now for the most important part of the story. I made it on time for my hair appointment. I was running 15 minutes early, the length of time I was helping the woman. Punctual people build unexpected delays into their schedules. I would like you, too, to pad your schedules for unexpected delays, unexpected time that you will take to help someone.

What waiver?

On yet another family outing at Oceano Dunes, Andrea*, Robert*, and I were riding rented quad runners at one end of the park. At one point we were on a narrow trail with a steep up-sloping dune to our right and the park barbed wire fence to our left. Robert was in front, Andrea was in the middle, and I was behind Andrea.

I don't know how it happened, but at one point I saw Andrea and her quad in the air. I stopped. It was like watching a movie in slow motion. *OK. I see a quad flying over the fence. And I see Andrea flying over the fence.* Fortunately, the two landed separately and on more sand.

I called Robert back and we hopped the fence. Even though Andrea wasn't very old, she was out of shape, so I had to lead her like I lead seniors in how to stand up. Plus, she was too heavy to lift in sand. Robert and I were able to put the quad back on its wheels. There was a slight up-slope from where the quad landed and the fence, so I held the fence down while Robert sat on the quad and floored it. He made it! The next challenge was to turn the quad away from the dune, dig it out of the sand, and head back to base camp.

We were able to get the quad fully functional, again, and Andrea was able to ride back. She wasn't hurt, fortunately, and we returned the quads without a whisper of the crash.

If the owner of the quads is reading this story, then you can assume the story is fiction.

I went camping with my friend Sherry* at Ocotillo Wells, a desert in San Diego County, California. One morning we set out on a hike, but it didn't go well. It was supposed to be a leisurely, flat walk: an hour out and an hour back.

Ten minutes into the hike, Sherry said, "Ah!"

"Are you OK?" I asked.

Sherry didn't know immediately. She just knew that she was in pain. Sherry looked down at herself and saw huge needles sticking out of her right hand and a huge chunk of cactus in her left, inner thigh. It turned out that she accidentally kicked up a chunk of round cactus that was about the size of a Nerf football. The cactus was kicked up to Sherry's hand and, as a reflex, she shook her hand, and the cactus was flung into her thigh. My eyes popped out of my head. I had my first aid kit with me, but what first aid tool pulls a chunk of cactus out of someone's thigh?

Sherry took off her shirt, which was no big deal because she always wore a jog bra. Being utterly modest, I was relieved that it wasn't my shirt. Why did it matter? We were in the middle of nowhere with no one else around. I wrapped the shirt the best I could around the cactus without poking myself. I knew that I had to get it right the first try. "Here we go!" I pulled, and the cactus came right out.

Step two. I pulled the needles out of the shirt, and Sherry put the shirt back on. Step three. I pulled the remaining needles out of Sherry's thigh, grabbing at the base of each and making a quick motion. Step four. I pulled about ten needles out of Sherry's fingers.

Step five. It was time to turn around and go back to the campground to treat the wounds and rest. Oh, no. You don't know Sherry. "I'm fine," she said. "Are you sure?" I asked, knowing what the answer would be. We finished the hike and I treated the wounds when we were back at our campsite.

Sherry is only five-feet two-inches tall, but her mind is as tough as her body. She is a mountaineer who climbed Mount Kilimanjaro and completed the 300-mile Eco-Challenge in Alaska. I'm not worthy!

I'm sorry, I don't speak Chinese

I used to frequent a Chinese restaurant where the day and time I showed up was as predictable as what I ordered. I appreciated the good customer service, including the workers remembering my order, and how quickly my meal was ready. Since my typical lunch time is 2 p.m., there normally wasn't anyone else in the restaurant.

One time that I walked into the restaurant, I saw four of the male employees, including the owner, standing in the middle of the business looking at things on the floor. Curious, I took a closer look and asked what was going on. It turned out that the owner purchased a cabinet that needed to be assembled. Even though the directions were in Chinese, in addition to English, the staff didn't know what to do.

Being a wood worker, that project was right up my alley, so I offered to help. The owner accepted. I took the directions and started moving hardware and wood around. They all kept telling me no no no. I didn't know what I was doing wrong. Did they want my help or not? They wanted my help—conditionally. They wanted me to read the directions and tell them what to do, but they wouldn't let me assemble. Why? Was assembling man's work? Did they want to be left with *some* ego in tact? I don't know.

I played along, and we completed the task in an hour. After, in true form of being a smart businessman, the owner offered my meal gratis. I accepted.

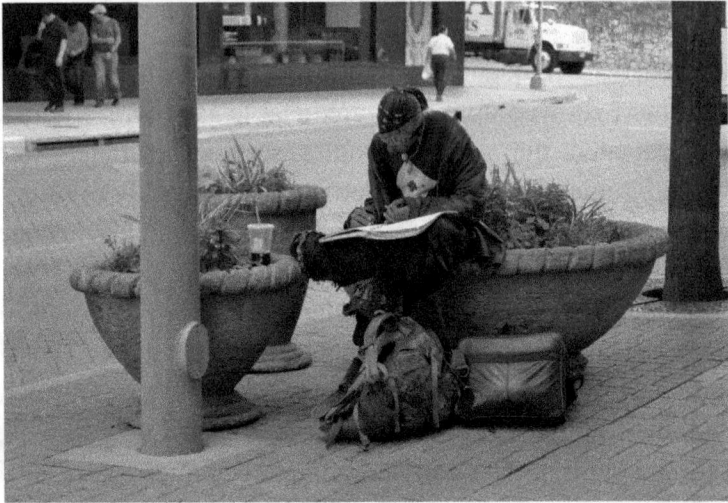

Who said that?

The Alamo. The river. The cavern. The insane. These are four components of San Antonio, Texas. When I was walking around town I came upon a man in his 20s (?) sitting on a planter drawing in his sketch pad. Since drawing isn't one of my skills, I am always eager to admire what other people create. Sensing that this man wasn't drawing with a full set, I approached cautiously.

"Hi. I'm Jeanne. Can I please look at your drawings?" The man handed me his whole sketch book. Most of the pictures looked like a study in human anatomy. I wasn't sure if his skill or unique mind were more fascinating. Judging by the notes on each page and the man's behavior, I decided that he was schizophrenic.

"These are beautiful [they really were]. You are so talented. Can I buy these three pages?" The man nodded. He tore out the pages. "Will you please sign and date them?" I asked. The man did, handed them to me, and signaled that he didn't want money. "Can I buy you something to eat?" He pointed to the nearby convenience store and told me what candy bar and soda to buy. *Sometimes I have to turn off my health expertise.* I bought the food and handed it to the man, who was grateful. I walked off with my new treasure.

I can't tell you enough how much I would like the man's artwork to display in this book, but I don't own the rights to it. I have no way of asking the man for his permission, unfortunately. I would so like to promote him, but for many people their art is not for public use, just to maintain or attempt sanity.

I hope that the man will forgive me if I made any erroneous assumption about him.

Open says-a-me

I love to take things apart and put them back together. It's fun to see how things work. Being mechanically inclined means that I can fix things on my own, not pay someone, and extend the life of objects past the point of what they were designed, these days. Tinkering also gives me logic to problem solve things I haven't studied before.

I walked into a university library and headed for the two elevators. They were the type with one door, each closed from the left. Standing by myself at the two doors on the first floor, I pushed the up button. I could see from the lights above the doors that the door on the right was taking its time coming down from the fifth (top) floor and the one on the left was about to touch down.

The elevator on the left displayed first floor, but the door was slow to open. Then it opened only a tinch. I could see that there were two people in the elevator waiting to walk out, but couldn't squeeze past the slight opening. I gave them several suggestions: "Push open. Push close. Push second floor." The elevator car stayed put and the door closed and then made a futile attempt to open and then it closed and barely opened again.

By this time, other people had walked up to use the elevators. I told them that the one on the left was broken and to use the one on the right. I had the opportunity to sail upward, but I was determined to rescue the two students. With the elevator door stuck partly open I told the two people, "I have an idea. Press close again." As the door shut, I quickly stuck my arm in and allowed the inner part of the door, the part with the sensor, to hit my arm. Then I quickly pulled my arm back out, and the door slid open all the way. The two people walked out and right past me. No pomp and circumstance. No Thank You. As my dad used to say, "He didn't say thank you, kiss my ass, or go to hell." As my yoga teacher friend would say, "You're not supposed to do things for others expecting anything in return." Screw that. Ha.

Off to the stairwell I went.

Not a fan of dirt

It's important to have a sanctuary, a safe place where you can be away from the stresses of the world. For some people, that place is in their homes or yards. For others, the "world" and associated stresses *are* at home. My sanctuaries tend to be at the top of a hill or mountain, where I sit and ponder, half-way through a hike, the meaning of life.

One such hill is in the town that I live in and takes an hour to hike to the top. Although this canyon trail is actually a dirt road, I rarely pass anyone on foot or in car. I love having trails all to myself! When I am at the top, I sit in the dirt for 30 minutes and look out at the beautiful view of the valley before hiking back down.

One time that I was at the top of the hill, I saw a really nice car coming up. Nice car? The driver's lost. The dirt road is so rough that only 4-wheel-drive truck owners willingly drive up it. At the point where I sit, there is a fork in the road. To the left is a private driveway, and to the right the dirt road continues along a ridge toward another canyon. I stood up to allow the driver to have room to go either way.

The driver stopped and motioned me over. She said, "Jeanne!" I said, "Wendy*!" Small world. Smaller town. We knew each other from networking. Wendy was frantic. She was not the off-roading type and was frazzled from driving that hairy road, being lost, and without cell reception to call for help or use GPS. Wendy said that she was trying to get to a party. I told her that I could either help her turn around or direct her to the way out via the ridge road. Wendy didn't like either choice, because both choices were off-roading—too scary for her.

I said, "I've been an off-roader for decades. I don't mind driving you out of here and to the party if someone will give me a ride back to my car." "Deal," Wendy said. She hopped out of the car and around to the passenger side. I sat in the driver's seat, and we took off. We had a nice time catching up, while Wendy decompressed from fear. It took us 10-15 minutes to get back to civilization and to where the party was. By the time we arrived, she had cell service and was able to call her husband to meet us at the house and take me back to my car. Then, he and I had a nice time catching up.

You see how helping people can get you out of exercising? I hiked an hour, rather than two hours. Hmm. That excuse should be in my publication *The Every Excuse in the Book Book: How to benefit from exercising, by overcoming your excuses*. Excuse #?: "I had to drive a lost person to a party." Ha. I should have helped Wendy on the way up; walking downhill is so much easier than up.

Number, please

I passed an ATM right after a woman had used the machine and walked back to her car. As she was sitting in her car with the door open, I said, "You forgot your receipt. Do you want it?" She said, "Yes." I said, "I'll get it for you." I pulled the receipt out of the machine and walked it over to the woman.

As I was walking toward her, I looked at the balance on her receipt and noticed that she had thousands of dollars in her account. I asked her if she could spare a few dollars, knowing that she clearly could and that she couldn't lie about it.

OK all of paragraph two is a lie. I couldn't help myself. Artistic license.

Bye

When I was door knocking in a senior neighborhood, I heard a woman struggle to yell, "Come in!" I had been door knocking long enough to know that either the home owner was expecting someone or couldn't get to the door and left it unlocked. It was the latter.

I slowly opened the door and peeked in, not knowing what I would find. There was a woman sitting on the couch in her living room converted to a hospital. She was quite sickly and struggling to breathe, but strong mentally. I introduced myself, and the woman invited me to come in and sit down on the other couch. I carefully maneuvered my way past all the machines and lines that were keeping her alive, barely. My mind sifted through a series of possible medical conditions as I attempted to diagnose, possibly lung cancer.

The woman wasn't too curious about my books and career; she mostly wanted to talk. I listened. In a nutshell she told me about her family and her whole life story. I stayed for about 15 minutes and then excused myself to get back to my route. As I was walking out, the woman said, "I'm not going to be alive much longer. I probably won't be here next time you're in the area." *Uhhh. So much for leaving on a high note. It breaks my heart when someone tells me that.* Yes, I had heard that before.

From September 1991 to December 1992, I lived in Honolulu, Hawaii, right after graduating from college. I immersed myself in the Hawaiian culture whole-heartedly. One social habit I noticed and subsequently practiced is that when strangers, acquaintances, and friends part ways, they say, "See you." I loved that. I loved the idea that it's

OK to part ways, because we will see each other again. "Bye" then sounded so final, so sad. *I'm never going to see that person ever again.*

When I left the old lady's house, I sided with reality. I turned back and said, "Bye."

Nut so fast

I was at a grocery store at the check-out behind an elderly gentleman. After he was finished and my items were being scanned, I noticed that there was a bag of pistachios on the counter. "Did the man leave the pistachios behind?" I asked the cashier. "Yes," he said plainly. *Don't go too out of your way to help a customer.* Stores cheat customers more than customers know, maybe to make up for theft. Hmm. Which comes first? Don't get me started on stores no longer being able to give coins as change. Yes, I'm willing to round up if the difference comes from <u>your</u> pocket.

I took my time checking out. How difficult can it be to catch up with an elderly man? When I was outside the store, I had a nice bird's-eye view of the parking lot below, but I didn't see the man. *Do I actually remember what he looked like? Maybe I wouldn't make a good witness after all.* I remembered how the man was built, slender. *Hmm. Maybe he is fit enough to move fast.* I walked up to one car with the door open and I could see a man in the driver's seat wearing shorts, obese, and with peripheral vascular disease. Not a match. *This guy won't live to be a senior.* Plus, I didn't really think my guy would drive a new Acura. I find that people who were either in WWII or grew up during that period don't buy products made by "Japs."

I walked to a different part of the parking lot and looked for an old, well-cared-for car. There it was: a little American-made truck backing out of a space with the elderly man in it. Poor guy. I almost gave him a heart attack, as I let him almost hit me so that he could see I wanted to talk with him. The man stopped and rolled down his window. I held up the bag of pistachios. "Did you leave these behind?" "Oh, yes, I did. Thank you," he said with genuine gratitude. The man looked as though his faith had been restored about "kids these days." I wish I could say the same.

Mexican fight club

I was in my truck in a convenience store parking lot late at night about to leave when three Mexican men caught my eye. They looked like they were landscapers who worked for the same company, as they were near two work vehicles and still wearing company uniform.

They started fighting—in slow motion. It was the strangest fighting I had ever seen. No, I didn't grow up in the 'hood, but I took boxing lessons twice—real boxing lessons, not foo-foo boxing. The men were clearly drunk.

The men were all hitting each other and alternating between two-on-one. Cell phones were being dropped, blood was splattering, men were on and off the ground. I wasn't about to break up the fight; *maybe I should take bets*. Ha. After about 15 minutes of *what am I watching?*, I called the police, waited for them to arrive, and told an officer what I saw.

I wasn't sure why I called the police. I didn't care if the men hurt each other. The officer informed me of why I called: We didn't need more drunk drivers on the road. *Oh, yeah, that.*

CHAPTER 4

CHILDREN

It's up to adults to protect children and to give them tools to be safe. Obviously kids are vulnerable. Obviously kids are special. Unfortunately, child cruelty is rampant. If we take time to protect only one age group, then it should be children.

Open your eyes and ears when you are around children in public. Signs of child abuse aren't hidden behind closed doors. Children not only need to be protected from traffickers but also, in some cases, the children's parents.

Make the most out of any time you spend with a child, no matter how long the encounter or how well you know the child. Teach them something. Say something uplifting. Listen.

I see you

Before realizing I am an empath and before fully understanding the gift (sometimes a curse), I misjudged people. One of my city-league softball coaches was a person I misjudged. I thought that he was a really nice person, a good person. Then, the blinders came off.

The man's wife and son came to the park to watch our games. I noticed that the man was particularly bossy with his wife, who was particularly passive. I really enjoyed the boy, who was about eight years old. The boy's disposition was that of an adult, like a little man. So cute.

One night when we were by the stands warming up, the man became irate with his son. He yelled at his son, and the boy ran down the stairs and hid under one of the benches. *Oh, my gosh. He's abusing his son.* I walked over to the boy and stood by him and stared down his dad. *I see you. I now see you for who you are. How dare you hurt a child. Not now. Not here. Not on my watch.*

It was fascinating to watch the man contain himself so as not to publicize what a horrible person he is. I knew, though.

Needless to say, I never played for that coach again. A few years later I crossed paths with the boy, who was with two friends. I heard how he was talking. Not nicely. The boy became an asshole. The boy became his father. Innocence lost. I didn't remind the boy who I was.

My fists make an impression

I was about to walk into a copy center when I heard a commotion. I turned around and looked back toward the parking lot. A boy about 10 years old was running back and forth around a car with a man watching. I stared to determine if they were playing or if the boy were in danger. Unfortunately, it was the latter.

The man was yelling at the boy to get in the car. The boy yelled back, "Daddy, no!" The boy was in sheer terror. The poor kid knew that no matter what he would be hit: in the parking lot, in the car, or at home. He had nowhere to go, no shelter, no sanctuary. I walked part-way toward them and yelled, "Leave him alone!" The man responded with obscenities. Not everyone should have children.

Outed as an abuser, the man quickly put his son in the car and drove off. I was angry and rattled. I walked into the store and told a worker what happened. He said, "Well, it's none of our business." I said, "Child abuse is everyone's business." The worker's response just made me angrier. *I have your number.*

Image by Jim Tyler

Old school

When I toured Pennsylvania on a road trip, traveling from Pittsburgh to Philadelphia, I had my roller skates with me. I love touring cities on my skates. It's a great way to get around and to see a lot in a short period of time. Also, skating is my way of connecting with the energy of my surroundings. Some people like to sit outside a cafe and drink coffee. I skate.

This trip I particularly wanted to skate in Lancaster County—Amish country. From what I had seen in pictures, the area looked like an outdoor skater's dream: miles of smooth asphalt and no cars. When I arrived I went into a visitor's center to get my bearings, pun intended. As I was walking out, a tourist magazine caught my eye. On the cover was a couple inline skating down a street. *What?!?!? How can that be?* I was planning on being the first person on the planet to roller skate in Amish country. I was so disappointed. To recover, I convinced myself that the photo was edited. *The lighting is all wrong. Those skaters were never here.*

I put my skates on in the parking lot and set out on my journey down to christen Lancaster's streets. I quickly found myself back in time with my '70s-style, white, boot skates not being as old school as the farm equipment on either side of me or the horse-and-buggies I passed.

At the end of a road and a T intersection, I came upon a one-room school house with a large yard where children were playing. It was the first time that I had seen such a school still in use. I stood at the split-rail fence in wonderment at these beautiful children in their "period" clothing, girls in dresses and white bonnets, boys in button-up shirts and pants with suspenders.

It didn't take long for the kids to notice me. They stopped their softball game and rushed a different section of fence. The ogler became the ogled. I waved and said hi. They were stone-faced and quiet. I waved again. Nothing. I asked, "Do you want me to do some tricks for you?" Nothing. I did anyway. I skated back and forth to warm up and then I did what's called a spiral (pictured). I stopped and looked at them. Nothing. Jeez. Tough crowd. Then I did a jump called a toe loop. I didn't stick the landing; I fell. They laughed and laughed and laughed. *Oh. They want _that_ kind of show.* I stood up and began a routine of improvised physical comedy, pretending to fall repeatedly. They laughed and laughed and laughed.

Wanting to reserve energy to get back to my car, I ended the show and bid adieu. They waved, I left, and they went back into the schoolhouse.

I went to a bar to listen to a band and to dance. After I was there for a little while, I saw six people walk in: a young couple, their two toddler daughters, and a set of grandparents. During the time they were there, they had so much fun. The young couple danced with their children, who were in dresses. Since the girls were twirling and being flipped, I could see that one was wearing shorts under her dress and one was just wearing underwear. I wasn't the only one watching the fun. There was a man in his 60s who was also watching—too intently, too longingly. Since a criminal psychologist had already taught me how to spot a pedophile, I recognized this man as such. It is a creepy thing to watch. They fixate, stare, and demonstrate a physiological, sexual response to children. It's disgusting and disturbing. I pulled the young mother aside and said, "You all look like you're having a lot of fun. I'm really sorry to be a downer, but I have to tell you what I see. That man at the bar is watching your girls in a bad way. I just want you all to be safe." She said, "I know. I saw it, too." They left.

What a shame that this asshole ruined the fun for six people—six customers the business lost. Maybe for good. That man is a regular. Unfortunately, I've seen him more than once. I haven't told this story to the owner of the bar, yet, but I want to.

Why were children allowed in the bar? I think it's the type where anyone is allowed in and drinkers are carded.

Filled to the rim

I was out of town visiting a friend of the family, a woman who was my parents' age. I had known the family since I was born, as we all had moved into the neighborhood right after the homes were built and right before I was born.

While I was visiting, my friend's daughter Ashley* stopped by so that I could meet her daughter Heather*. I knew that Heather had emotional issues, but I didn't know exactly what they were or the source. I just knew that I needed to make the biggest impact I could on this child during the little time that I had with her.

I said to Heather and Ashley, "Meet me at the end of the driveway in five minutes." They did. In the cul-de-sac I put on a roller skating show for them. Heather, just four years old, had never seen anything like it. She was wide-eyed and all smiles. When I was done I skated up to Heather and knelt right in front of her. "Can I put my hands on your arms?" She nodded.

I put my hands on Heather's upper arms and looked her right in the eyes. "You are a beautiful girl. I enjoyed meeting you and spending time with you. I hope we get to meet, again, soon. OK?" She nodded.

I didn't say much verbally, but I communicated a lot through touch. I gave Heather my energy so that she could feel love as a possible antidote, if only temporary, to whatever distress her soul was experiencing. It worked. Her little body quivered from bottom to top and she smiled from ear to ear.

It's been years since I've seen them; I hope everyone is doing well.

Duck!

I was at a park exercising on the playground equipment with my friends' kids. There were a lot of people around, but the playground wasn't crowded. At one point I rested and looked around, as I am always surveying my surroundings.

I saw a boy about five years old walk in front of the swing set. *Oh, no.* He was totally oblivious to the danger. *He's going to be kicked in the head. Where are his parents?* Sure enough, the boy was accidentally kicked in the head by one of the swingers. He was knocked down and started crying hysterically. A woman and I ran over to the boy. The woman swooped him up and ran him over to where she was sitting; I followed. Since neither the woman nor the child spoke English, and I didn't speak Armenian, it was difficult for me to help, but she seemed to be comforted by my being there.

The boy stopped crying and just stared off. Since I didn't know the boy, I wasn't sure what his baseline was. I sensed he was a little off to begin with. Since the mother was calm, and the boy was soothed by her rocking, I decided I wasn't needed anymore.

Snitch

I was standing at the back of my truck in a parking lot behind a building, stretching after a walk. I saw two teenage boys and one teenage girl sitting on a bench by the building. No one else was around. The kids looked like they were behaving themselves, but something told me to keep an eye on them.

About five minutes into my stretches, a car pulled up fast and parked crooked near me, and a man in his 50s jumped out of the car. The kids bolted. Once on the sidewalk, one of the boys caught up with the other boy and starting pummeling him. The girl screamed for the boys to stop. They finally did and ran off in separate directions.

The man yelled at the girl to get in the car. She yelled back that she wouldn't. After they yelled at each other a few more times, the girl ran off and the man drove away.

I called the police and waited—an hour—to give my report. An hour! Was I in Los Angeles? No. I was in a small town—where the police department was across the street!

What I figure happened is that one boy sent a text to the girl's father to tell the father where she was. When the father showed up, the other boy beat up the first boy for contacting the man.

How was I a Good Samaritan? I'm not sure that just calling the police qualifies as Good Samaritan, but acting on a premonition that something bad is going to happen does.

Creepy

I was at a pizza parlor where I went into the women's restroom, which had two stalls. Just one other girl and I were in the bathroom and she was in a stall crying hysterically. I could tell that she was not using the toilet, just on the phone with a friend. She kept saying, "Come get me." I had already seen the girl sitting in a booth with two men, one in his 60s, the other in his 70s.

I stayed by the sink until the girl came out of the stall. She looked like she was about 17 years old. I asked her what's wrong.

She said, "Nothing, I'm fine."

"What's going on?"

She vacillated between hysteria and strength. "I'm fine."

"Is someone hurting you?"

"No, no. It's nothing like that."

"What's going on? Who's hurting you?"

"No one."

"Is your dad hurting you?" I assumed that the younger man in the booth was her dad.

"No, my dad would never hurt me." That was the only thing I believed. In other words, her dad would never hurt her and neither man in the booth was her father.

"I can help you."

"I'm fine. I don't need help."

After about 15 minutes in the bathroom with the girl, there was a knock on the door. It was the younger man. I peeked out and told him to wait. I told her to take her time coming out of the bathroom and that I would talk to him.

I left the bathroom and spoke to the man. I fully opened myself to absorb his energy and to assess his intentions. It was scary to feel him—very creepy. I told him that she would be right out. Through my words I pretended like everything was fine. "You know girls take a while." But, I gave him a look of: I'm onto you.

He said, "She gets like that a lot." RED FLAG.

The girl finally came out of the bathroom and sat at the booth with the two men. I could tell they were about to leave; meanwhile, I walked out of the restaurant. I sat in my truck and called the police. I told the dispatcher what I saw in the restaurant and who was getting into what car. The girl drove off by herself, and the men followed her in another car. I gave the dispatcher the license plate numbers and the direction of their travel.

The dispatcher asked if I saw a gun or knife. I said no.

"Did you see anyone hurt someone else?"

"No, but—"

"Did you see or hear anyone threaten to hurt someone else."

"No, but—"

The dispatcher said that there was no reason to send police to the scene or to pursue the vehicles. *Oh, but there is reason to send police to the park when I am dancing by myself to no music?* So much for Protect and Serve. AND, we're supposed to report when we think we see proof of sex trafficking, which is what I thought I was witnessing, but the police didn't act. These men would have been an easy pick.

Unfortunately, this was also a case where you can't help someone unless they want to be helped.

Executive decision

Pictured on the top of the previous page is Zion National Park as seen from the (almost) top of Angel's Landing trail. Below that image is a railing at the edge of a cliff in Bryce Canyon National Park. Hopefully, you can tell from both images that I was pretty high up. When I took the Zion photo, I was standing by a railing but I didn't photograph it for the purpose of this story as I did the Bryce railing. The Zion railing's lower horizontal bar was half-way down the vertical bars and there was no fencing.

I saw a seven-year-old boy at the edge of the Zion cliff step in front of me, put his hands on the top bar, put is legs over the middle bar, sit on the middle bar, and then start to put his head under the top bar. In other words, he almost had his whole body on the other side of the railing. I said, "No!" and grabbed the boy by the collar and pulled him back on the safe side. "Where were his parents?" you ask. The boy's dad was standing right next to us and said nothing to me or his son. His dad just gave me a vacant look. The boy was totally unfazed, too, and resumed sight-seeing. A couple of minutes later, I heard the boy ask his family, "Do you think if I fell I would die?" You see why adults need to look out for kids? It takes a long time for logic to kick in. I'm still waiting for logic to kick in for the boy's dad.

One of the reasons why I made this executive decision was because I think about the gorilla who was shot and killed after a boy fell into the animal's pen. When parents aren't parenting, other present adults need to step up. I believe that there were plenty of adults at the zoo catastrophe who could have held back the child.

Angel's Landing. Yes, there was an angel up there that day.

Cammy to the rescue

Can I share one of Cammy's Good Samaritan stories? We were at the park (same as two snake stories) walking around during little league games. The park was hoppin'. While we were walking back to the car, we stopped at the water fountain on the side of the bathroom building right next to the parking lot. Cammy was off leash, because he listened better, and Tommy was on leash.

Tommy stepped up to the water fountain for a drink and then stepped down. Cammy stepped up to the water fountain, and then a 3-year-old girl stepped up and pushed the button for Cammy to drink. We had never met the little girl before. Cammy and the girl's interaction was so cute; my boys loved children and were protective of them.

All of the sudden Cammy's head popped up, he thought for a second, jumped down, and then bolted around to the other side of the bathroom. *What is going on?* Tommy and I gave chase and found Cammy attacking a dog that was walking with its owner. I pulled Cammy off and put his leash on, and then I put both in my car. Several people saw what happened and looked at me like I was the most evil person on Earth for having a "vicious" dog. One woman cried, "What if it were a child?!" Ugh! The ignorant. If only there were a delete button for them.

I'll never know what Cammy sensed, but I do know one thing for sure: Cammy was protecting the little girl at the water fountain. There were other dogs at the park, but Cammy didn't act defensively until this particular dog arrived on scene. Dogs, and animals in general, are more perceptive than we will ever be, and we should trust their judgment.

Number 1 rule

At a bookstore I used the restroom, which had two stalls. I wasn't sure if anyone were in the other stall; the door was closed, but I couldn't see any feet. While I was washing my hands I heard, "Mommy! Mommy!" I looked around. I don't know why. It was a small bathroom and clearly no one else was in it.

I asked the little girl, "Do you need help?"

She said, "Yes."

I looked outside the bathroom and didn't see Mommy, not that I knew what Mommy looked like. There wasn't anyone around.

I went back in the bathroom and said, "I don't see Mommy. What do you need?"

The little girl said, "I need help wiping." *Oh, no.* Having babysat from when I was 10 to 24 years old, I had had my fair share of wiping bottoms, seemingly more than an actual mother, and I was done with it—especially after a child goes number 2.

"Can you open the door?" I asked.

The little girl opened the door. The child was two or three years old. "Did you just go pee pee or caca also?"

"Just pee pee."

I know I'm a safe person, but the last thing I needed was a mother walking in and seeing me touch her daughter's private parts.

I instructed the child how to wipe, helped her pull up her pants, and then helped her wash her hands. I walked out of the bathroom to help the little girl find her mother. Immediately, the child ran up to her mom, who had a couple other small children in tow, unfazed that one had wandered off for a potty break. I walked off without saying anything to the child's mother.

CHAPTER 5

STRUCTURES

Being successful in helping others and convincing others to accept your aid not only requires confidence but also feigning that you know what you're doing. At age 17 when I was teaching swimming lessons for my first time for pay, my boss gave me my class schedule, which included back-to-back groups of children and one group of adults—fearful (of water) adults!

What?! I have to teach adults, fearful adults?! That wasn't in the instruction manual. I was actually excited and up for the challenge. I incorporated the same teaching techniques on them as I did children, using slightly different language. My adults practiced everything my kids did: blew bubbles, bobbed, kicked, floated. Before having one man go under water, he asked, "What are you going to do if I have a heart attack under water?" My eyes popped out of my head and then I calmly responded, "I'll bring you back up, pull you onto the deck, and begin CPR." He said, "OK," and went under water . . . and came back up on his own.

The point is: fake it if you have to. Learn by doing. Swimming lessons became a service in my health and fitness business; fearful adults became my favorite group to teach how to swim; and the service and demographic became the most gratifying of my whole career.

Say it isn't so

You know the feeling you have when you're driving home and there is an emergency vehicle with its lights on in front of you heading in the same direction? *Please don't let it be my house.* That's not what happened. Ha. Close. I was driving home and was viewing a large plume of smoke. *Please don't let it be my house.*

While I was driving I hoped the smoke wasn't coming from my neighborhood. Farther along, I found it was. Then I hoped the smoke wasn't coming from my street. Farther along, I found it was. Then I hoped the smoke was not coming from my house. Farther along, I found it <u>wasn't</u>. Phew. I drove past my house considering the possibility that the large fire was going unnoticed by everyone but me. I found the house from where the flames were shooting up. *Maybe no one is home.* I drove up the long driveway and found cars parked. *How could they not know that there is a massive blaze in their backyard?* I parked my truck and knocked on the door.

"Hi. I'm Jeanne. I live down the street. Did you know that there is a massive fire in your backyard?" "No," the man said. We bolted around his house to the backyard and found his large chicken coop on fire. Somehow the flames hadn't touched the house, yet. The man called the fire department, and I ran back to my truck to get my fire extinguisher. Back at the coop I just stood and stared. "Don't bother," the man said. Yes, I knew I didn't have enough defense.

When I heard the fire truck sirens I took off. The fire was started by a space heater in the coop. All of the chickens died. The moral of this story is: some people shouldn't own animals.

Goodbye, deposit

I was door knocking when I saw flames shooting above a nearby house. *I hear no sirens and see no emergency vehicles, so Jeanne to the rescue!* I bolted down the street and around the corner and found where the flames originated. There was a huge fire coming from a backyard. I set down my books and pulled myself up on a fence to look over. People were casually standing in the backyard looking at the fire. I said, "It's coming from that room."

I was wrong. The fire was coming from the gas BBQ. The large flames + wind + closed windows caused an optical illusion. The flames were going toward the house and bouncing off the back wall and windows. Realizing such, I yelled, "Turn off the gas." A man yelled back, "I did."

I watched for a few minutes as the flames subsided. It was weird watching the six people mesmerized by the flames and paralyzed.

I went back to door knocking. I never did hear sirens.

I was sure that the house was a vacation rental. *They won't be getting their deposit back.*

I was tempted to knock on their door, but I didn't have hot dogs for sale.

CHAPTER 6

DREAMS

I am an empath, a highly sensitive person (HSP), and an intuitive. You can think of empath as empathy; although similar they are not the same. Let's start with sympathy, which is feeling compassion for what someone is experiencing. "I feel sorry for him." Empathy is feeling compassion for someone by way of having had a similar experience. "I know what it's like to lose a grandparent." An empath is someone who can feel other people's emotions to the point of those emotions becoming one's own. For example, when someone gets irate and yells at me, I feel his anger and become scared. Since I infrequently feel my own anger, and never rage, feeling others' anger is rattling and scary. It sucks the life out of me and it takes a while for me to re-ground.

An HSP is someone who senses energy more than what most people perceive. Everyone can sense energy. Think of the times that you felt someone looking at you and you turned around and saw that someone was. Also, there were times that you were thinking about a friend and then that friend called. You said, "I was just thinking about you, and then you called." This happens to me all day, every day.

Everything is energy: emotions, feelings, thoughts, objects, space, beings. As an HSP I can sense all of the above. That's a lot to take on, right? Believe me, I know. I have to meditate and do yoga regularly. There have been times when I've walked into a business and thought: *What just happened? Someone was yelling.*

An intuitive is similar to intuition, which is knowing something without being told. You don't know why you know; you just know. If you're a parent, especially a mother who carried (i.e., pregnancy) the child, you know what I mean. You know when something is wrong with your child, even if the child is not in the same room with you. An intuitive is someone who has these experiences to the nth degree and has premonitions though intuitives wouldn't necessarily consider themselves psychic. I don't consider myself a psychic.

I not only intuit events when I am awake but also when I am asleep. I have had so many premonitions come true, which I have shared with the people who are in my dreams, that people not only request I tell them *every* dream about them—good or bad—but also they request I dream answers to questions they have about their lives. On rare occasions I will ask for answers for others, but you don't have to be gifted to receive your own answers. Your Higher Self is as all-knowing about you just as The Higher Source is all-knowing about the universe.

I *sometimes* misunderstand what people say, I *rarely* misunderstand body language, I *never* misunderstand what people feel.

Infected

I had a friend whose sister was in a hospital's intensive care unit, due to sepsis, a whole-body bacterial infection that causes multi-organ system failure. She was close to death multiple times, but still hanging in there when my Mom (deceased) gave me a message in a dream.

My Mom said, "Sam's* sister needs to start a new medicine regime, soon, so that it is completed by March." I passed the message to Sam, who said, "The new medication was started."

It's my understanding that Sam's sister finally recovered from her illness.

An interesting side note to this story is that I received another message, this time while awake. I had a great uncle whose wife was born in Ireland. After her mother died young, my great aunt and her sister were sent to England to be raised by other family members. (I don't know about their father.) The message was that Sam's sister was my great aunt's mother reincarnated. I wrote Sam's sister to tell her of my epiphany, risking the possibility that she would think I'm a real nut job.

In the letter, I wrote that the two children went on to live wonderful, healthy lives with beautiful families of their own. Since we can bring unresolved issues from past lives into subsequent lives, I connected Sam's sister's illness with guilt that my great aunt's mother presumably had for not surviving long enough to raise her children. The moral: MOST diseases and pain have an emotion component. It's NOT "all in the genes."

I didn't hear back from Sam's sister.

[Whoa. Several months after having written this story, now editing this book, I am having a flash about "March." Since this story happened in 2018, I thought March meant March 2019. Now I realize my mom meant March 2020—when the coronavirus kicked in. Wow. Sam's sister needed to be well and out of the hospital to avoid being a casualty of the coronavirus. Whoa.]

At the time of the following dream, there were a lot of riots and protests happening around the country. My dream was a foreshadowing of protests developing in my area.

I have a client who owns a shop in a city-center. I dreamt that he was wearing his cowboy boots while climbing up the wrong side of a metal, A-frame ladder. My client was also angry while on the ladder, because he was resentful about the protests and concerned about the safety of his store and employees. His anger caused him not to be careful and his feet slipped down three steps while the ladder fell toward me. My client said, "Grab it." I did. He stepped down safely.

Immediately following this dream, I had the same dream. After I caught the ladder a second time, I (still in dream state) told my client about the first dream. He said, "You should have told me." The next morning I wrote my client an e-mail telling him briefly about the dream and to please be careful. I also said that my dreams don't necessarily manifest literally, so just be careful in general.

I had the dream on a Monday night, Tuesday I wrote the note and worried about him all day, and Wednesday I not only received a response from him but also heard that protests began in my area.

Thursday I saw my client for a scheduled appointment. I told him the dream in great detail. My client asked, "When did you have the dream?"

I said, "Monday night."

My client said, "Monday I was on a ladder to fix something at the edge of my home's roof. I stood on the top step, even though I knew better not to. The ladder fell, and

I was left dangling from the roof. I was able to get down without hurting myself, luckily."

My mouth was agape hearing this story.

My client said, "After I read your e-mail, yesterday, I made a point to be careful when I was on a ladder, again."

My client was on a ladder, again, this time in front of his business—to clean the security camera lens. Why? Protestors!

"Please let me know of every dream you have, good or bad. I don't want to be left in the dark," my client requested.

Pressured

I dreamt that I was coming down an escalator in a convention center. No one was around, except my friend's husband, Carl*. I could see him walking ahead of me in the hall, his back towards me. Carl was grabbing his head with his hands by his ears. He was having a stroke.

The next morning I had to decide whether or not to honor the pact I had with my friend, also an intuitive. *Do I have to tell her <u>this</u> dream?* I told her. My friend said regretfully, "Oh." We weren't too surprised, because her husband was a highly stressed, unhappy person.

Six months later my friend called me to tell me she was about to fly to Europe. Her husband had a stroke while on a trip abroad. Carl survived the stroke but, as is common, he had another. I predict that there will not only be another stroke but also that that stroke will kill him.

The more often I talk with someone, especially in person, the more energetically connected I am with that person, and the more likely I am to dream about him.

Two such people, married couple Bob* and Lisa*, I normally see at their office, so the dreams normally take place there. In one such dream the three of us were standing chatting near their reception desk. They both told me that they had been feeling dizzy, Bob more than Lisa. Lisa said that she felt mildly dizzy after turning suddenly while standing. Bob told me that he had been severely dizzy to the point of having fallen twice and hit his head once.

In the dream I was about to tell them what I thought the dizziness meant, but I didn't get a chance to. So, in real life I told them about the dream and what I thought it meant. I said, "The western medicine side of me could come up with plenty of causes of dizziness and tell you to go to the doctor, but you don't even have that symptom in real life. The eastern philosophy explanation makes more sense anyway: you're out of balance. You're off balance. You don't have balance in your lives. Your lives are too heavily weighted on working and taking care of others, rather than yourselves. You need to take this message to heart, because if you don't take more time for yourselves, then you'll get sick."

They said, "You're right. We're even thinking about retiring." I wanted to do my I-knew-it dance, similar to my I-love-being-right dance, but I shouldn't celebrate being right about something negative.

When I saw Bob and Lisa two weeks later, they told me that in the following month they would be out of town on a two-week road trip. No reservations. They were just going.

Of course I gave myself credit for their taking a vacation. I also had to give them credit for heeding my encouragement to create balance in their lives.

Lass, come home

I dreamt that my friend Debbie's* elderly, sickly parents were trying to communicate with Debbie. It was November, and my dream included Debbie's mom writing Debbie a letter asking Debbie to come home for Christmas, because she didn't know how much longer she would live.

The two families lived on opposite sides of the country, so Debbie getting to her parents' house was not only challenging for Debbie with a husband and two kids but also unusual for her to do during the holidays. I told Debbie about the dream and said, "Just consider it."

Debbie didn't go back east, and Christmas 2018 and another has since passed. Debbie's parents are still living. At the time of my dream, I explained that my dreams aren't necessarily in the same time-space continuum that we experience in our conscious lives. "The scenario could be this Christmas or another one in the future."

[Update: Debbie's dad died right after Thanksgiving 2020. As I type this, she is driving out to see her mom.]

CONCLUSION

I don't help people and animals for the money, though I wouldn't turn it down. I don't help for the glory, though I would jump in front of a news camera. I don't help to be the star of the next viral video, though I wouldn't turn down a media tour. I help because that's the right thing to do—the humane thing to do—one of the main reasons we are on Earth, the most difficult school in the universe.

Some people believe that humans are either altruistic or selfish. Even though I am a black and white thinker, I don't agree. No human and, according to my college zoology professor, no animal is altruistic. There is always benefit to helping others, the least of which is that it feels good. Is helping with the intent of getting a buck selfish? I don't think so. As an entrepreneur I see that as enterprising. Not taking the time to help someone is selfish and not helping because you don't think you'll get paid is bad karma.

I don't think that I have ever been offered money or material gift for one of my Good Samaritan acts. In the past I wouldn't have accepted compensation, but now I would. I realize that although I was not taught the myth that money is the root of all evil, I was taught to turn down financial or material gratitude. It's really important to accept gifts so as not to deny the giver the joy of their actions.

You're getting the idea that if Armageddon occurs you'll want me around. I can stay calm in chaos, when everyone else is hysterical. No, I'm not always cool. I sweat the small stuff. For example, I freak out if I drop a slice of bread on the floor. Do you know how much that cost?! I eat gluten free!

ABOUT THE AUTHOR

Entrepreneur Jeanne "Bean" Murdock brings a unique approach to storytelling, fusing writing, comedy performing, and photography. Performing on roller skates where she can, her improvised physical comedy is one that has never been done before. Jeanne's sassy, naive perspective wins audiences' attention, demanding that "the show must go on."

A unique aspect of Jeanne's photography stems from being an empath–someone who can perceive the energy of living and non-living things. As a result, each image is a translation of what she feels from the subject. Each image is also a depiction of Jeanne's state of mind at the time and her opinion of the subject. Those three variables result in quite a recipe for visual art. Jeanne's portfolio is a documentary of her travels.

Jeanne is a prolific writer, penning screenplays, books, and of course her own jokes, to name a few.

Originally from Cupertino, California, Jeanne was given the nickname **Bean**, in third grade by her next-door neighbor, simply because it rhymed with Jeanne. She studied physical education at California Polytechnic State University in San Luis Obispo, and then started **BEANF**IT Health and Fitness Services in 1992. In 2014, Jeanne stopped offering health and services, but retained **BEAN**FIT for her brand of books.

Image by Jim Tyler, edited by Greg Heller

Qualifications:
California Polytechnic State University, San Luis Obispo
<u>Bachelor of Science in Physical Education</u>: concentration
 in Commercial/Corporate Fitness
Graduation Date: June 1991

San Diego State University, San Diego, CA
<u>Nutrition Didactic Program</u>
Verified: May 2002

Questions? Comments? Please feel free to write or call Jeanne "Bean" Murdock anytime at:

PO Box 1083
Paso Robles, CA 93447
Phone: 408-203-7643
Website: www.JeanneMurdock.com
E-mail: laugh@JeanneMurdock.com

Other books by Jeanne "Bean" Murdock
(via BEANFIT Publishing):

*The Every Excuse in the Book Book: How to Benefit from
Exercising, by Overcoming Your Excuses*
*Successful Dating at Last! A Workbook for Understanding
Each Other*
*It's Hard to Find Good Help These Days: A Customer
Service Manual for Businesses*
*That's a Bunch of Quackery! How to Avoid Being
Pick-pocketed by Misleading Claims in the Fitness
Industry*

Co-author of Carole Breton's autobiography
My Guardian Angel Wears Antiperspirant
(Stinky Ghost Cat Books 2018)

Not-so ghost writer of Ted Gilbert's autobiography
Barefoot NOMAD
(POGA Publishing 2019)

www.ingramcontent.com/pod-product-compliance
Lightning Source LLC
Chambersburg PA
CBHW060901280326
41934CB00007B/1146

* 9 7 8 0 9 7 7 0 6 7 8 6 2 *